Flavored Butters

NUTS ◎ DAIRY ◎ HERBS ◎ FRUIT

Flavored Butters

NUTS ☙ DAIRY ☙ HERBS ☙ FRUIT

Offerico Maoz

TEN SPEED PRESS
Berkeley | Toronto

Ten Speed Press
P.O. Box 7123
Berkeley, California 94707
www.tenspeed.com

Distributed in Australia by Simon & Schuster Australia,
in Canada by Ten Speed Press Canada, in New Zealand
by Southern Publishers Group, in South Africa by Real
Books, and in the United Kingdom and Europe by Airlift
Book Company.

Design by Catherine Jacobes Design
Photography by Danya Zigdon
Butter mold and stamp photographs from Butter Molds
    & Stamps, by Barbara S. Van Vuren and Robert E. Van
    Vuren (www.buttermold.net).
Photograph on page 2 by Elan Penn.
Photograph on page 4, "Betty at the Churn," by the Allen
    Sisters, circa 1904. Courtesy of Pocumtuck Valley
    Memorial Association, Memorial Hall Museum,
    Deerfield, Massachusetts.
Edited by J. E. Sigler

Library of Congress Cataloging-in-Publication Data
Maoz, Offerico.
    Flavored butters : nuts, dairy, herbs, fruit / Offerico Maoz.
        p. cm.
    Includes index.
    ISBN-10: 1-58008-694-2
    ISBN-13: 1-58008-694-3
    1. Cookery (Butter) 2. Butter. I. Title.
TX759.5.B87M36 2005
641.6'72—dc22   2004026819

First printing, 2005

Printed in China

1 2 3 4 5 6 7 8 9 10 — 09 08 07 06 05

Contents

*"Eat butter first and eat it last and live till
a hundred years be past."*
—DUTCH PROVERB

BUTTER AROUND THE WORLD

Even though our word for butter comes from the Greek word *boutyron* (literally, "cow cheese"), butter actually goes back much further than even that ancient civilization. The Bible is one of our oldest references, and it often makes mention of butter as a staple in the ancients' diet and as a symbol of richness and comfort. While it is uncertain whether or not it was the biblical Hebrews who discovered butter, it is clear that the Mediterranean region was also the birthplace of butter. And archaeologists suspect that it was not born by accident: either by stirring cream too often or by dragging it behind an animal while traveling over rocky terrain, ancient peoples quickly learned that liquid milk can be turned into thick, creamy butter. The earliest methods of making butter—that we have knowledge of—use just that sort of technique: milk was placed in an animal skin, which was then sewn up and agitated one way or another, either by dragging it behind a horse, swinging it back and forth from tent poles, or just tossing it around. (Making butter has always been a fun chore for kids.)

In the Middle East, many Arabs still make butter this way today, and in Mexico native peoples were still dragging butter behind their horses at the turn of the century. In other parts of the world, however, people began contriving all sorts of contraptions to improve what was essentially the churning process early on. About 4,000 years ago, ancient tribes in India were

the first to begin fashioning primitive churns. As these advanced butter-making techniques caught on farther north and west, we find that everyone from the Egyptians, Romans, and Greeks to the medieval Europeans and up to the American colonists contributed something to the development of churning technology.

Just as important as the churning was the preservation. After all, butter is pretty easy to make, but keeping it fresh and free from bacteria in the prerefrigeration age was something of a challenge. Butter was tightly wrapped in everything from cabbage leaves and freshly cut grass to cow dung and was often salted. In colder regions, such as northern Europe and Scandinavia, locals packed butter into barrels called firkins, which they then promptly buried in the ground. The structure of the firkin and the coolness of the soil prevented the butter from going rancid for prolonged periods of time, and, much like wine, the flavors of the butter developed and matured while buried, thus becoming even more delicious with aging.

In warmer climates the environment was less accommodating, and the butter itself had to be altered. Southern Asians were the first to clarify butter, a cooking process that separates the milk solids (the part of butter that goes rancid) from the butterfat, which could be preserved for several weeks even without refrigeration. Clarified butter is still the preferred form in Asia and many parts of Africa, and its advantages are now well appreciated in European, especially French, cuisine.

Surprisingly, butter is actually an important staple in many countries in the East, and in many parts of southern Europe it was once considered a disgusting food of the uncouth northerners. It is true that in Japan most people are still lactose intolerant, and the term "butter stinker" is still used to describe the most strange and foreign (Western) people, ideas, and things. Butter is relatively low in lactose, however, and since the 1960s the Japanese have been gaining a taste for the creamy dairy delight that Europeans have enjoyed for centuries.

Butter is not only a food, but has been used as a cosmetic, as a medicine, as insulation for the body against the cold and as personal bug repellent, as lamp oil, and for oiling the body when bathing was a luxury. It makes very frequent appearances in the national and religious festivals of the world, and it is even an artistic medium, used for carving sculptures and reliefs from Tibet to Minnesota.

In Hindu culture, where the cow is considered holy, ghee (clarified butter) is held to be its sacred gift to the people. It is offered as food to the gods, is burned in holy lamps, is used as medicine and sacred oil in religious ceremonies, and is the primary animal fat used for eating and cooking, either pure or mixed with the milk of water buffalo. Boys are initiated into manhood with ghee, and images of the gods are even washed with this purest of holy substances.

Samna, as clarified butter is called in the Moslem world, is made from sheep and goat milk and is an integral part of many traditional dishes. It comes seasoned and spiced with herbs and spices such as cinnamon, cardamom, turmeric, rosemary, and thyme and with sweeteners such as honey and dates. In the south of Morocco, it is traditional for farmers to bury a pot of spiced clarified butter on the day that a daughter is born, so that it may be dug up and served atop the couscous at her wedding feast. Even in Ethiopia, one of those localities in which butter was once considered a repulsive substance eaten only by barbarian foreigners, nit'r k'ibe (spiced clarified butter) has become the proud heritage of generations (see page 98).

The United States had a rich colonial butter culture, and today butter is still celebrated at dairy festivals, offering city slickers an opportunity to milk, churn, paddle, and taste. As hard as we've been on butter in the last few decades, the United States is still the number-one producer of butter in the world, churning out about 1 billion pounds a year.

TRADITIONAL HOMEMADE BUTTER

We buy our dairy products at the supermarket today, but butter was traditionally made in the home. Up until the early twentieth century, butter-making in the home was considered such an important part of family life

that, in 1908, more patents were issued in the United States for "new and improved" home butter churns than for any other new contraption. For our great-grandmothers, preparing the butter, from milking to spreading, was a weekly chore; these days most of us don't even know how butter is made.

Until the whole process became industrialized, making butter was (in most parts of the world) the exclusive prerogative of women. The word "dairy" derives from the Middle English word for "maid," which originally meant "bread kneader." Milking and making cream, milk, butter, and cheese—and bread— consumed a considerable amount of pre-modern woman's time, but in time, she became quite expert at the skill, and the results of her labor were as appreciated as they were vital to the sustenance of her family.

To make just one pound of butter, she needed twenty-one pounds of fresh whole milk. She allowed the milk to sit untouched, usually in a lot of shallow dishes, until the cream rose to the surface. She skimmed off the cream, collected it into a pail, and then, if she was making what is known as "sweet butter," transferred the cream directly to the churn and started turning. Churning separated the liquid in the cream (which is buttermilk) from the semisolid fat (the butter), and she could tell when they were separated by the feel of the crank as she turned it; the butter would "break," and suddenly the smooth turning became a sloshing (the buttermilk) with a lot of coarse, grainy resistance (the butter globules). At this point she drained out the liquid and poured in some water to wash the butter. She then turned some more, drained out the water, added more, turned again, drained, and added until the water poured out clear instead of cloudy. The washing simply removed any residue of buttermilk, which would prevent the butter from solidifying. Then she transferred the butter, which was still a lot of grainy little globs, to a flat surface and worked it with a pair of paddles or some other tool in order to press out more buttermilk. Once all clean of liquid, she continued to work it until it took on the proper texture and usually salted it to preserve it.

TYPES OF BUTTER

Butter can be made from practically any type of milk or cream, and there are butters on the market made from soured milk, from soured cream, from the whey produced during cheese processing, and from a variety of animal milks, mostly cow, goat, and sheep.

Sweet (Cream) and Cultured Butters

In Europe, cultured butter is preferred to sweet butter (also called sweet cream butter) because the bacterial culture that's added to it rounds out the flavor of the butter, giving it fuller texture and a richer, slightly tangy taste. In America, sweet butter is preferred, though cultured butter is becoming more popular. It is often labeled "European-style butter" instead of "cultured," but it's the same thing.

Typically, cultured butters are unsalted, though even if they are salted, they still contain much less than the average American butter. Sweet butters were originally so-called because they contained no salt, though they weren't noticeably sweet. These days, however, there is confusion between "sweet butters" (unsalted) and "sweet cream butters" (may or may not be salted), so just know that most American butters labeled "sweet" in any way are in fact salted, and too heavily for my taste. (They can contain up to 2 percent salt.)

Unsalted and Salted Butters

Salted butter has a longer shelf-life (about five months instead of three), because salt acts as a preservative. Salting masks unpleasant odors, and it is harder to determine the freshness and quality of butter when salted.

I almost always call for unsalted butter in my recipes. If you must use salted butter when I call for unsalted, leave out the salt in the recipe, at least until you've tasted the prepared butter. As a general rule, cook with unsalted butter and keep the salted variety for spreading. One more thing about butter labels in America: if they don't say whether or not they're salted, they *are* salted.

Whipped Butter and Butter Spreads

Whipped butter is intended to be used as a spread. Even when it's cold, it's easier to spread than nonwhipped butter because it contains more moisture and air. I will never call for it, though, for several reasons. First, all of my recipes really require you to whip the butter yourself, because you add things to the butter as you whip it. Second, whipping butter yourself at home is easy, and it tastes much better. Third, the whipped tub butters (and any other butter labeled as a spread) contain much less fat than regular butter, as well as added water and frequently other vegetable oils. This makes them much easier to spread, but entirely unsuited to cooking. They will throw off your results in my recipes, as well as any other recipe in which you try to incorporate them. Finally, while some butters are simply beaten with air, others have nitrogen and other gases whipped into them to give them more volume. They're not necessarily harmful, but why add something like that to your diet when you don't have to?

THE "MOO FACTOR"

Aside from these pretty commonly known variations, there is another factor that seasoned chefs and old-fashioned churners know is even more important. This is a difference that is determined prior to churning: I like to call it the "moo factor." It should be pretty obvious that the quality, content, color, and taste of butter depend upon the milk from which it's made, and the composition of the milk naturally depends on the cow that gave it. There is a whole science of variables that influence the cow's milk production, some of the most important being the species of cow and the cow's diet, "lifestyle," and environment.

Yellow and Pale Butters

The primary difference produced by the "moo factor"—and the one you can tell a lot by—is the color of the butter. Butter hues are generally simplified and broken into two large groups: yellow butter and pale butter. Yellow butter is more common in the summer, when cows are more likely to graze in open fields. In the winter, when fresh grass is rare and cows often feed on stored hay, we usually get paler butter on the shelves. Yellow butter contains less milk solids and more butterfat, while pale butter has it the other way around. This makes yellow butter slightly richer and more buttery-tasting, with flavors varying from "beefy" to those of fresh grass and nuts. Pale butter tastes slightly milder, with flavors varying from fresh asparagus to the taste of warm milk on a rainy day. For the average person, though, the difference is very, very tiny, and even chefs make more of the color than the flavor.

Both yellow and pale butter are used in cooking and baking. Most chefs use the milder-flavored pale butter for making sweet butter-creams in order to ensure that the flavor of the butter does not overpower the other delicate, sweet flavors. Also, since butters turn

Cream, heavy cream, and buttermilk.

even paler when beaten, pale butter becomes practically white, and this resemblance to whipped cream makes it the preferred butter for topping, frosting, and decorating. It is also most often used for white sauces, such as beurre blanc (white wine butter sauce), because it leaves the sauce pale and fair. Yellow butter is usually used in frying, sautéing, and baking, because its rich flavor is enhanced by heat and especially by slow cooking. It makes pastries flakier, baked goods crumblier, fried foods crunchier, and so on.

As for butter in stick or tub form, I recommend you use the sticks for this book, but only because they're easier to measure and so generally more convenient for following recipes. Butter in opaque packaging, such as aluminum foil, waxed paper, or thick tubs, is preferable to others because butter is very sensitive to light (which causes rancidity) and easily absorbs unwanted odors and flavors if not properly wrapped.

How to tell if you've got a good-quality butter? At room temperature, it should be dense with no air bubbles or lumps, it should look creamy and smooth without any stickiness or brittleness, and it certainly should not sweat. If you look at it and still aren't sure, taste it. Rancid butter tastes sour if it went bad on the counter; if left too long in the refrigerator it takes on a stale refrigerator taste.

MODERN HOMEMADE BUTTER

Today you can make butter at home with food processors, so it's easier than ever. Follow these simple instructions to make butter in your food processor. The amount of butter you'll get will be about half the amount of cream you start with. Ideally, cow's cream should be about 60°F when you start; goat's milk, 55°F. You will definitely notice a difference in the flavors of homemade versus store-bought butter.

Fill a food processor about one-quarter to half full with heavy whipping cream. It's the agitating that counts, so it doesn't really matter which blade you use. Process for several minutes, until the butter "breaks" and you clearly see a liquid (the buttermilk) separated from a solid glob (the butter granules). You'll see the following stages: thick liquid, airy foam, soft whipped cream, firm whipped cream, grainy whipped cream, then a sudden collapse of the cream's form, a few seconds of sloshing, and the final separation.

Pour out the buttermilk (into a jar if you want to drink it). You can taste the butter at this point (or even take it out and eat it, but it will keep better and have much better texture if you continue). Add ice cold water, about one-quarter the original amount of cream. Process for a minute or two, then drain the water. Add the same amount of clean cold water, process, and drain. Continue adding and draining water until it pours off clear.

Transfer the butter to a smooth, hard surface or a cool bowl and work out the remaining liquid. A potato masher works best for this, but you can use two forks, the back of a spoon, little paddles, or even just shake it in a jar. Pour off the water now and then, working the butter until it is the texture you want. If you like, add a few pinches of salt at this stage and work them in.

You can also whip the cream on low speed in a blender. Or, if you have some patience, shake the cream by hand in a tightly closed jar (this takes 5 to 30 minutes, depending upon the energy of the shaker).

Storage: Butter can be kept at room temperature for about a day, or in a butter crock on the counter for several weeks. In the refrigerator, it will keep for about a month, but be sure to put it in the coldest part of the refrigerator, not in the door (which is usually warmer). In a regular freezer it will last 4 to 6 months, in a deep freezer below −10°F, up to a year. If you decide to freeze a few batches of homemade butter, remember that freezing intensifies the flavor of salt in butter and alters its moisture content and texture; it should be just fine for cooking, but never bake with any butter that has been frozen.

If you're uncertain whether or not your butter is still fresh, you can check it by cutting off a small slice. If the inside of the butter is the same color as the outside, it's still good. If the outside of the butter is darker than the inside, the butter has oxidized and should be discarded.

MAKING FLAVORED BUTTERS

In general, it's best to make flavored butter in a cool room. If you're working in a warm climate, turn on an air conditioner or avoid working during the hot hours of the day.

While most flavored butters can be left at room temperature for several hours, bacteria begin to multiply as soon as butter reaches room temperature, so it's best to keep it in the refrigerator. Store all flavored butters in airtight containers in the coldest part of the refrigerator (the door is warmer), away from light and any strong odors (such as lemon, onion, and garlic). Also, even though butter might keep for weeks and sometimes even months, the other ingredients in a flavored butter have their expiration dates as well,

inches for putting on large entrées such as steaks, and so on. Cylinders can be stored in the refrigerator or freezer. To cut off coins, dip a very sharp knife in hot water and slice little rounds off the cold butter, immersing the knife again to heat whenever necessary.

To dice butter, remove it from the refrigerator, place it in a square pan about 1 inch deep, and let it soften at room temperature. Use a rubber spatula to flatten out and smoothe the surface of the softened butter, then cover it with plastic wrap and refrigerate for 40 to 60 minutes, until the butter is completely cool and hardened.

Remove the plastic wrap and dip the bottom of the pan into a bath of warm water for 1 to 2 minutes, then turn it over onto a hard, flat surface and dice the butter with a very sharp knife. Store the cubes either in a single layer on a large plate covered with plastic wrap or stacked into layers separated by waxed paper in a bowl with a tightly fitting lid.

Savory Butters

Savory butters (which include spicy, salty, and seafood butters) often contain acidic ingredients such as vinegar, wine, tomatoes, lemon,

so consider them when choosing a recipe to make in advance. Almost every flavored butter tastes best closest to the time of preparation, so if you want the very best flavor, use it up within a few days.

To make a cylinder, place a batch of butter on a wide sheet of plastic wrap, fold the far edge over toward you, and firmly grasp all the edges. Roll the butter back and forth a few times in order to shape it into a sausage-like roll. The thickness of the roll should be appropriate to the food you want to use the coins with: a diameter of one inch is good for slipping into sandwiches, one and a half and so on. It is therefore very important to prepare these butters in a nonreactive bowl made of wood, glass, plastic, enamel-coated clay, or—least preferably—stainless steel, which tends to react with some substances, especially acidic ones.

Use only very fresh ingredients when making savory butters. If you must substitute dried herbs for fresh, remember that 1 tablespoon fresh herbs equals 1 teaspoon dried. Onions, green onions, shallots, and other sharply flavored ingredients develop strong odors caused by oxidation if chopped hours in advance, so chop them right before you need them.

Storage: While it is usually recommended to wrap butter in aluminum foil to protect it from light and strong odors, the acidic ingredients in savory butter might react with the foil. Therefore, wrap it in waxed paper, plastic wrap, or an airtight glass jar or bowl.

At room temperature, these butters keep for up to a day in a cool, dark place. They keep up to 2 weeks stored in an airtight container in the refrigerator and up to 4 weeks in the freezer. Covering the butter with a layer of plastic wrap laid right on its surface, as is done with avocado to prevent browning, can preserve it for a couple more days.

Nut Butters

I've included a few real nut butters to this collection in order to provide some nondairy options (see All-Natural Peanut Butter, page 52, and Hazelnut Butter, page 56). Real nut butters taste incredible right after preparation, especially if you roast the nuts yourself at home. You'll also notice there are a lot of "nut butters" that are dairy; these are regular savory butters that just feature nuts and should be used, stored, and served just as a savory butter.

Storage: You can store nut butters at room temperature in an airtight jar for 1 to 2 weeks or in the refrigerator for up to 3 weeks. Homemade nut butters have no preservatives and are very high in fat, so they will go rancid if kept too long. They are far more perishable than store-bought peanut butter.

Sweet Butters and Buttercreams

Sweet butters are just like savory butters but contain sweet ingredients in place of (or in addition to) acidic ones. Buttercream is a simple combination of butter and sugar beaten together until very pale and fluffy. The beating eliminates greasiness and incorporates air, resulting in a lovely rich, frothy substance that resembles whipped cream. Buttercreams can be made either with eggs or without, but because it's a long and complex procedure, I decided to prepare all my buttercreams without eggs for this book.

Sweet butters should also be mixed in nonreactive bowls and with a wooden spoon. Buttercreams are beaten on medium-low speed until all the ingredients are well incorporated; then speed is increased to medium-high until the mixture has doubled in volume.

Storage: It is best to use both sweet butters and buttercreams immediately, but they will keep up to a week in an airtight container in the refrigerator. A sweet butter can be frozen for a week as well, but a buttercream's delicate texture will be altered by freezing, and so it should only be refrigerated.

Butter Sauces

Butter sauces are sauces that are thickened with the addition of butter, usually at the very end of cooking. Typically, the liquid ingredients in the sauce are cooked until reduced by one-third to one-half the original amount; then cold, diced butter cubes are whisked in over very, very low heat. Using very cold butter and extremely low heat is important because butter sauces separate easily. Using cold butter helps cool the sauce as it's being whisked in, which helps incorporate the butter and prevents separation.

In most of my butter sauce recipes, I call simply for "stock." Traditionally, a sauce is made with chicken stock if it will be served over poultry, with veal stock if it's to be served over red meat, and with fish stock for seafood dishes—but if a different combination tastes good, go for it.

Storage: There is no good way to store a butter sauce. Let it sit for over 20 minutes, and it separates into melted butter and mush.

COOKING, BAKING, AND FRYING WITH BUTTER

Usually, you should use softened butter in cooking and baking, and you'll use it for most of the recipes in this book, too. To soften refrigerated butter, let it stand at room temperature until it reaches 65° to 70°F (about 30 minutes to 2 hours).

If you're in a hurry, there are three other ways to soften butter quickly. One way, ideal

BUTTER	CUPS	GRAMS	POUNDS	TABLESPOONS
1/8 stick	1/16 cup	14 grams	1/32 pound	1 tablespoon
1/2 stick	1/4 cup	56.5 grams	1/8 pound	4 tablespoons
2/3 stick	1/3 cup	75 grams	1/6 pound	5 tablespoons + 1 teaspoon
1 stick	1/2 cup	113 grams	1/4 pound	8 tablespoons
2 sticks	1 cup	227 grams	1/2 pound	16 tablespoons
4 sticks	2 cups	454 grams	1 pound	32 tablespoons

for pastry dough, is to whack it with a rolling pin. Or you can place the butter in a double boiler or a bowl over a steaming pot or kettle for 1 to 2 minutes. Microwaving the butter on medium heat for 10 seconds is an option, but it tends to separate liquids from solids, and once that happens in butter, there's no way to get them back together. If you must use the microwave, open it every 2 seconds to check if the butter is soft enough.

Frozen butter should be thawed in the refrigerator overnight, then handled just like refrigerated butter. (Never bake with butter that has been frozen, though, as freezing changes the taste and texture.)

Cold butter is often used in pie crusts, in some pastries, and in butter sauces. Cold but-ter should be taken directly from the refrigerator and incorporated into the mixture before it has had time to warm or soften.

Butter is also an excellent fat in which to fry and sauté, but its greatest advantage—flavor—can be tricky to preserve. The melting range of butter is narrow (from 82.4° to 96.8°F), and you've surely burned it once or twice. Put the butter in the skillet before placing the skillet on the stove. Butter burns instantly when placed in a preheated pot, so always put it in a cool one. Melt slowly, over low or medium heat, and fry or sauté over medium heat, unless otherwise specified.

Do not use any reduced fat, spreadable, or whipped butters, which are intended solely for spreading. These are usually labeled "not

vitamin A and also contains calcium, phosphorus, and vitamin D. Yes, it's high in saturated fat, but your body does actually need a limited amount of even saturated fats, and children in particular need quite a bit in order to grow properly. It's also not as high in cholesterol as many people think and, *eaten in moderation,* certainly poses no danger to healthy people on normal diets.

Flavored butters make great gifts. You can find a large variety of old-fashioned butter tools, like stamps that were used for decorating squares, butter crocks used to preserve butter on the counter, and hand-held churns from the midtwentieth century, all of which make a great gift packed into a basket with a few cylinders or little bowls of butter.

intended for cooking and baking" and often come in a tub. They contain added water, air or gases, and vegetable oils (which make them easier to spread) and so yield inferior results.

Margarine and other butter substitute spreads and substitutes might be good for spreading and use in recipes that specifically call for them, but for general cooking use and the recipes in this book, they simply are not up to par.

If you're health conscious, let me assure you that butter is an energy-rich source of

Savory Butters

Artichoke Butter

This recipe uses a French cooking method called confit, in which the food is covered with a layer of fat and simmered over very low heat until cooked through. It takes a little time, but not much effort, and the result will simply melt in your mouth. Fresh artichokes are obviously best, but they are a bit more work, and frozen ones do work pretty well in this recipe.

PREP TIME: 60 MINUTES, PLUS 8 HOURS
    CHILLING

5 artichokes

1 tablespoon freshly squeezed lemon juice

1 cup unsalted butter

2 cloves garlic, peeled

1 sprig dill

1/2 teaspoon salt

Remove and discard all artichoke petals. With a small, sharp knife, trim the stem to about 3/4 inch; use a small spoon to scoop out the hairs on the heart. Rub both the stem and the heart with the lemon juice to prevent browning. Thinly slice and transfer to a saucepan.

In a separate saucepan over low heat, heat the butter until just melted. Pour over the artichokes to cover completely. Add the garlic, dill, and salt. Cook over medium-high heat until almost boiling, decrease the heat to low, and let simmer for about 40 minutes, until the artichokes are very tender. Remove from the heat and let cool in the saucepan for 15 minutes.

Transfer to a food processor fitted with the metal blade and process until very smooth. Refrigerate in an airtight container overnight. Bring to room temperature before serving.

Serving Suggestions

This is a delicate spread that complements the subtle flavors of gourmet food very well. Serve on foie gras or calf livers or atop steamed or poached white-fleshed fish or seafood.

Honey-Mustard Butter

They say opposites attract, and in this case they're right. The contrasting flavors of honey and mustard are precisely what make a seemingly awkward match so incredibly popular. In this interesting triangle, the sharp, hot flavor of the mustard is softened by the natural sweetness of the honey as well as the smooth, fresh milkiness of the butter.

PREP TIME: 10 MINUTES

1 heaping tablespoon honey

2 tablespoons good-quality prepared mustard

1 teaspoon white wine vinegar

1 teaspoon Worcestershire sauce

1 cup unsalted butter, softened

In a mixing bowl, combine the honey, mustard, vinegar, and Worcestershire. Mix well with a wooden spoon. Add the butter and mix until thoroughly blended.

Serving Suggestions

Put a little twist on the traditional Thanksgiving turkey by rubbing it with this butter before roasting. Or lightly flour chicken breasts and fry them in this butter.

Incorporate 2 tablespoons of the butter into 1 pound warm mashed sweet potatoes.

Peel new potatoes, place them in a frying pan with 3 tablespoons of this butter, cover with a tight-fitting lid, and roast over low heat for 15 to 20 minutes, until the potatoes are golden and tender. Don't forget to shake the pan from time to time in order to evenly coat the potatoes with sweet and spicy perfection.

Blue Cheese Butter

The variety of blue cheeses is almost endless: English Stilton, French Roquefort, Italian Gorgonzola, and countless other equally delicious American and international varieties. Any of them will do just fine for this recipe. If you want a more strongly flavored butter, use a mature blue cheese; fresh blue cheeses will produce a milder result. In this butter, I prefer a matured, tangy blue cheese, such as fourme d'Ambert. Note that the higher the fat content of the cheese, the smoother your butter will be.

PREP TIME: 10 MINUTES

1 cup unsalted butter, softened
1 cup blue cheese, at room temperature
Cracked black pepper

In a mixing bowl, combine all the ingredients, adding the pepper to taste. Use a fork to crumble the blue cheese and work it into the butter. Once the cheese is well crumbled, continue blending together with a wooden spoon until you have a fairly smooth paste.

You can also use a food processor to make this recipe. Combine the ingredients in a food processor fitted with a metal blade and process until smooth.

Variation: Blend 1 tablespoon finely chopped fresh chives into the butter for a little extra bite. If you are using a food processor, blend in the chives with a wooden spoon after the butter is smooth.

Serving Suggestions

This butter makes a great upgrade for sandwiches, toast, and crackers.

Try rubbing a whole chicken with this butter and then roasting to perfection.

If you make your own puff pastry, substitute this butter for half the amount of regular butter to give the dough extra cheesy flavor. It's the perfect enhancement for all your savory delicacies.

When making lasagna, try enriching your béchamel sauce with 2 to 3 tablespoons of this tangy butter.

Buttery Avocado Spread

Avocado is a truly wonderful fruit. Because it's very high in fat, it has a firm, smooth, buttery texture that melts in your mouth; but unlike butter, that fat is mostly unsaturated and very healthy. I prefer the Haas (California) avocado, which you can tell by its distinctive, almost black, grainy skin and relatively small seed. Its texture and flavor are remarkable, and no addition of fat is needed when this creamy avocado is used in a spread.

PREP TIME: 10 TO 15 MINUTES, PLUS 2 HOURS
      CHILLING

**4 ripe but firm avocados, skinned and
   seeded**

**2 scallions, green parts only, roughly
   chopped**

**1 tablespoon freshly squeezed lime
   (or lemon) juice**

1 tablespoon olive oil (optional)

1 tablespoon chopped fresh cilantro

1/8 teaspoon ground cumin

1/2 teaspoon salt

Pinch of sugar

In a food processor fitted with a metal blade, combine all the ingredients and process until very smooth. Taste and adjust the seasoning, if necessary.

Transfer the spread to a nonreactive bowl and cover with a piece of plastic wrap laid right on the surface of the spread to prevent browning. Refrigerate for at least 2 hours to allow the flavors to develop. Serve chilled.

This buttery spread will keep in the refrigerator for up to 3 days, if covered as instructed. After that, it will begin to turn black and lose its fresh flavor. So eat up!

Variation: Spice it up a little by adding 1/8 teaspoon chili powder.

Serving Suggestions

This spread is perfect on a fresh roll or bun all by itself, or as a sandwich spread. It is also wonderful as a thick sauce for a simple salad of very ripe tomatoes.

This spread is also great as a bed for freshly sautéed seafood. Try spreading it onto seared filet mignon as well.

Cheddar Butter

One of the most popular cheeses, cheddar has a wide range of flavors and sharpness that lets you keep making this recipe again and again without ever getting bored. Choose your favorite variety of cheddar first just to get familiar with this rich, creamy butter, then try all the rest. You can even substitute other types of semifirm cheese for the cheddar.

PREP TIME: 10 MINUTES

1 cup unsalted butter, softened

1 cup tightly packed shredded cheddar cheese

1 teaspoon hot pepper sauce (such as Tabasco)

Pinch of salt

In a food processor fitted with a metal blade, combine all the ingredients and process until almost smooth. Take care not to overprocess: the cheddar should retain some of its grainy texture throughout the smooth butter.

Serving Suggestions

For a delightful evening snack, dollop onto fresh-popped popcorn and toss to melt.

For an addictive cheddar shortbread appetizer, work the butter into 2 cups all-purpose flour and 1 1/2 cups self-rising flour, form into walnut-sized balls, and bake at 325°F for 15 to 20 minutes, until golden. Serve hot or at room temperature.

For an interesting twist on macaroni and cheese, toss pasta with lots of softened cheddar butter and serve with a big green salad.

Garlic-Dill Butter

The perfect harmony of garlic and dill makes for such smooth, subtle flavor that this recipe can be used even in gourmet dishes—but you're more likely to find yourself snacking on crackers spread with this butter all day. After two days, the herbs will begin to brown and lose their fresh flavor and aroma, so always use up your herb butters quickly.

PREP TIME: 5 TO 10 MINUTES

1 cup unsalted butter, softened

2 tablespoons chopped fresh dill

2 cloves garlic, chopped

1/2 teaspoon salt

In a mixing bowl, combine the butter and dill and mix well with a wooden spoon. Add the garlic and salt and mix until thoroughly combined. Taste and adjust the seasoning.

Variation: To bring out the flavor and color of the dill even more, make this butter in a food processor. Simply place all the ingredients in a food processor fitted with a metal blade and process for 5 minutes. Instead of little green dashes of flavor, the entire butter will turn bright green and burst with the fresh pungence of dill.

Serving Suggestions

Unexpected guests? Spread this butter onto some crackers and serve.

For a stellar side dish, cut 4 potatoes into wedges, spread out in a baking pan, dollop on 2 tablespoons of softened garlic-dill butter, and roast at 350°F for 20 to 30 minutes, until golden.

In a frying pan, combine 2 pounds fresh mussels or clams, 2/3 cup dry white wine, and 3 tablespoons of this butter, cover, and boil for 3 to 4 minutes, shaking the pan from time to time to mix up the juices. The shellfish are done when the shells pop open. Discard any shells that do not open. Serve immediately.

Garlic-Parsley Butter

The simplest combinations are sometimes the best ones. Use a rich-tasting, yellow butter and freshly peeled and crushed garlic—not the frozen minced garlic from the supermarket. Trust me, it makes a difference. As for the parsley, either flat-leaf or curly will do just fine. If you've never tried this with escargot, you should. Every snail lover knows that those delicious mollusks are best drizzled, dipped, or drenched in melted garlic-parsley butter.

PREP TIME: 10 MINUTES

1 cup unsalted butter, softened

3 tablespoons finely chopped fresh parsley

4 cloves garlic, crushed

$1/2$ teaspoon sea salt

In a mixing bowl, combine all the ingredients. Using a wooden spoon, mix together for 2 to 3 minutes, until the salt has dissolved. Taste and adjust the seasoning.

Serving Suggestions

Garlic butter can liven up any of your everyday breads: try it on bagels or English muffins for breakfast, fresh sourdough or pumpernickel for lunch, biscuits or rolls with dinner.

For an irresistible French garlic bread, slice a baguette and spread the garlic butter on each slice, then wrap the slices in aluminum foil and heat at 350°F for 7 minutes. The baguette will crisp, and the soft center will burst with the mouth-watering aromas and flavors of garlic, parsley, and butter.

Toss freshly cooked pasta in this butter and serve with meat, poultry, or seafood that has been dolloped with it as well.

Garlic-Herb Butter

Although many butter recipes are called "herb butter," this recipe incorporates a wide variety of fresh herbs to give the butter intense—almost extreme—flavor and aroma. You can use this recipe to create your own herb butter with your favorite blend simply by substituting different herbs, but there are two important guidelines: dried herbs should be used only in a pinch (remember that 1 tablespoon fresh herbs equals 1 teaspoon dried), and strongly flavored herbs (such as rosemary, sage, and marjoram) should be added or substituted only in very small amounts so that their flavor does not overpower the rest of the herbs.

PREP TIME: 5 TO 10 MINUTES

1 cup unsalted butter, softened

1 tablespoon coarsely chopped fresh chives

1 tablespoon coarsely chopped scallion, green parts only

1 tablespoon coarsely chopped fresh spearmint

1 tablespoon coarsely chopped fresh basil

1 tablespoon coarsely chopped fresh parsley

1 tablespoon coarsely chopped fresh dill

1 tablespoon coarsely chopped fresh tarragon

1 tablespoon coarsely chopped fresh chervil

1 tablespoon coarsely chopped fresh cilantro

1 teaspoon coarsely chopped oregano (fresh or dried)

1 clove garlic, crushed

$1/2$ teaspoon salt

In a food processor fitted with a metal blade, combine all the ingredients and process for about 5 minutes. Taste and adjust the seasoning.

Serving Suggestions

This butter is suitable for almost every savory dish. Use only a small amount, though, because its flavor is very strong. Upgrade meat or fish by dolloping on this butter before grilling, roasting, or broiling or by sautéing in it.

Dollop onto fresh grilled or boiled corn on the cob and let it melt.

It is naturally wonderful on fresh bread and rolls for breakfast. Spread on warm toast and serve with scrambled eggs fried in the butter.

Kalamata Olive–Herb Butter

Kalamata olives are almond-shaped Greek black olives that have been soaked in a wine vinegar marinade and then packaged in olive oil or vinegar. They have an almost fruity flavor, but are also very salty, so be careful not to overseason the butter. This butter is also particularly attractive when rolled and cut into coins; try serving thick slices on a platter at a party, surrounded by minitoasts and crackers.

PREP TIME: 5 MINUTES

1 cup unsalted butter, softened

1 cup pitted, finely chopped kalamata olives

1/2 teaspoon finely chopped fresh thyme

2 small oil-packed anchovy fillets (preferably Greek), chopped (optional)

Freshly milled black pepper

In a mixing bowl, combine all the ingredients and mix thoroughly with a wooden spoon.

Serving Suggestions

Cut off thick coins from the rolled butter and use in Greek—and all your other—sandwiches. Dollop on freshly baked sourdough bread with some sun-dried tomatoes and tangy, ripe goat cheese, then place under a broiler for just a few minutes. (This is a real favorite among my friends.)

Try as a seafood topping: dollop onto raw scallops, then place under a broiler (set to the highest temperature possible) and cook for 2 to 5 minutes, depending upon the size of your scallops, until scallops are medium-rare to medium. (Check doneness by poking them with a fork or knife.)

The butter is great for finishing Mediterranean sauces containing tomatoes or balsamic vinegar.

Lemon Butter

Lemon butters are used to give a dish the fresh, vivid scent and tasty tang of citrus. I often add basil, and I have friends who add a pinch of sugar, dill, lime or orange zest, pepper, and capers. Whenever a recipe calls for grated lemon zest, remember that the yellow zest of the lemon is where all the flavorful, aromatic oil is stored. The white pith beneath it is very bitter, so be careful not to grate it off, too.

PREP TIME: 5 MINUTES

1 cup salted butter, softened

Grated zest of 2 lemons

2 tablespoons freshly squeezed and strained lemon juice

In a mixing bowl, combine all the ingredients and blend with a wooden spoon until well mixed.

Variation: Add 3 tablespoons of finely chopped fresh basil, dill, or other herb, or capers.

Serving Suggestions

To make my favorite meal ever, I dollop lemon butter on a bed of pumpkin risotto and let it melt slowly. I serve it with fish or seafood that has been seasoned with 1 tablespoon lemon-basil butter and salt and pepper and baked until done. I follow up with a cheesecake made with lemon butter. You might try this meal in a little cabana hut—it's downright tropical.

When frying milk-fed veal scaloppine, replace the butter or oil with fresh lemon butter. You might never go back to plain butter again.

Mushroom Butter

The coupling of butter's smooth flavor with the full-bodied texture of the mushroom is a combination almost everybody appreciates. I use simple button mushrooms, but fresh portobello, porcini, and shiitake mushrooms are also good choices.

PREP TIME: 20 MINUTES

2 cups mushrooms

1 cup unsalted butter, softened

1 small onion, diced

1 teaspoon sugar

1 teaspoon salt

Freshly milled black pepper

1 clove garlic, crushed

2 tablespoons finely chopped fresh parsley

Brush and wipe the mushrooms to remove dirt. (*Never* rinse mushrooms before cooking; they readily absorb large amounts of water that will end up watering down your dish.) Use a very sharp knife to thinly slice the mushrooms, then finely chop the slices.

In a skillet over medium heat, melt 2 tablespoons of the butter and add the onion. Sauté for 3 to 4 minutes, just until the onion turns a very pale golden.

Add the mushrooms, increase the heat to high, and sauté for about 7 minutes, or until most of the liquid has evaporated and the mushrooms have turned a pale golden brown. Remove from heat and immediately add the sugar, salt, and pepper. Taste and adjust the seasonings.

Transfer to a mixing bowl, add the garlic and parsley, and mix well with a wooden spoon. Taste again and adjust the seasonings, if necessary. Set aside to cool at room temperature.

When the mixture is completely cool, add the remaining butter and thoroughly mix together with a wooden spoon.

Serving Suggestions

For a great starter, sauté goose or chicken livers in this butter, then chop them into tiny pieces and serve on minitoasts, accompanied by crème fraîche or sour cream.

For a delicious change of pace from plain old tomato sauce, boil spaghetti as usual, then toss with 2 tablespoons of the butter and 1/4 cup chopped fresh parsley, season with salt and pepper, and serve.

Green Peppercorn Butter

Green peppercorns are usually found preserved in vinegar, brine, or salt. They're very mild in flavor—you can even eat them whole right out of the jar—so you don't have to worry about a fire drill with this butter. The combination of green peppercorns and brandy works surprisingly well and so is widely used in many cuisines around the world. Definitely give this one a try, if only to familiarize yourself with this classic blend.

PREP TIME: 15 TO 20 MINUTES

2 tablespoons green peppercorns, drained (discard liquid)

4 shallots, finely chopped

1/4 cup good-quality brandy

1 cup unsalted butter, softened

1 teaspoon Worcestershire sauce

1/2 teaspoon salt

Pinch of sugar

In a small saucepan over medium heat, bring the peppercorns, shallots, and brandy to a boil. Decrease the heat to low and simmer for 5 to 10 minutes, until shallots are translucent and the liquid is reduced by two-thirds. Remove from the heat and let cool completely in the saucepan.

Transfer the peppercorn mixture to a food processor fitted with a metal blade and add the butter, Worcestershire, salt, and sugar. Process until almost smooth, but be sure to keep a bit of the grainy texture that is the peppercorn's hallmark.

Serving Suggestions

This is an excellent butter for quick-frying milk-fed veal scaloppine, sautéing pork or veal chops, or dolloping on filet mignon. Serve with a big baked potato dolloped with this butter as well.

Make a quick green peppercorn and cream sauce by melting 2 tablespoons of the butter in 1/4 cup cream and seasoning with salt and pepper. Served over juicy steaks, this sauce is sure to delight.

Parmesan-Bacon Butter

The smoky aroma of bacon blends perfectly with the sharpness of well-matured Parmesan and fine, milky butter. Get the very best ingredients you can find: Italian Parmigiano-Reggiano (or another well-matured, high-quality Parmesan) and high-quality, thinly sliced smoked bacon.

PREP TIME: 20 TO 25 MINUTES

4 ounces very thin slices smoked bacon

1/2 cup unsalted butter

Cracked black pepper

4 ounces Parmesan cheese, finely grated

Salt (optional)

Cut the bacon into very small strips. Divide into two batches and set aside one in a mixing bowl.

In a skillet over medium heat, melt 1 tablespoon of the butter and add half the bacon. Season generously with cracked black pepper and fry for 3 to 5 minutes, until golden and crispy. Remove from the heat and scrape into the mixing bowl with the unfried bacon, including the bacon grease. Let cool completely.

Add the Parmesan and remaining butter and thoroughly combine the ingredients with a wooden spoon. Taste and adjust the seasoning, if necessary. (Bacon and Parmesan are both pretty salty by themselves, so you probably won't need any salt. But just be sure.)

Variation: Add 1 teaspoon chopped fresh sage with the Parmesan and mix well.

Serving Suggestions

This butter is great in both cheddar and egg sandwiches with thin slices of cucumber. Or spread onto small crackers or minitoasts and serve as an appetizer. (You might want to make two batches for this one.)

For croutons, drizzle the melted butter onto fresh bread cubes and bake at 350°F for 5 to 10 minutes, until golden and crisp.

Soften the butter at room temperature and spread a *very* thin layer onto rolled-out puff pastry. Roll out again, then roll the pastry up into a cylinder, like you would a roulade. Use a sharp knife to slice off rounds 1/2 inch thick, place them on a baking sheet, and bake at 400°F for about 7 minutes, until golden. Serve warm as an appetizer, snack, or savory treat for company.

Pesto Butter

So easy and yet so incredibly rewarding. This butter is as diverse as pesto itself, but it adds refreshing, cooling dairy flavor to all the pesto dishes you already love. Of course, it's best to use fresh, homemade pesto, but you can easily find excellent pestos in Italian delis and larger supermarkets these days.

PREP TIME: 5 TO 10 MINUTES

1 cup unsalted butter, softened

$^1/_2$ cup pesto

Pinch of salt

In a mixing bowl, gradually add the butter to the pesto, 1 tablespoon at a time, mixing well with a wooden spoon after each addition. It's important to add gradually and mix thoroughly to avoid having the mixture become runny, forming a layer of melted butter on the surface. Once refrigerated, the melted butter will harden into a layer of unattractive yellow fat that cannot be blended into the rest of the mixture. So take your time and blend well. Once everything is thoroughly blended, add the salt, then taste and adjust the seasoning, if necessary. Serve at room temperature.

Serving Suggestions

Spread in mozzarella and cheddar sandwiches with slices of fresh, ripe tomato.

Rub a whole chicken with pesto butter and roast until golden and crispy. Or fry fish fillets, thin chicken breasts, and all kinds of meats in the melted butter.

Freshen up leftover pizza by dolloping on 2 teaspoons pesto butter and reheating.

For incredible, fresh dinner rolls, roll out raw canned biscuit dough to $^1/_2$ inch thick and spread with a thin layer ($^1/_8$ inch) of this butter. Roll into a roulade and cut into 1-inch coins, place on a baking sheet, sprinkle with a little freshly grated Parmesan, and bake at 350°F for 7 to 10 minutes, until golden.

Soy Sauce, Lemongrass, and Ginger Butter

This recipe was given to me by a colleague who cooked for several very successful restaurants that fused the flavors of East and West, where it was always one of his biggest hits. Lemongrass, ginger, and soy sauce are especially common ingredients in Southeast Asian cuisine, but the addition of butter is Western. Be careful if you've never worked with fresh ginger; it is very potent, so wash your hands after handling it and don't get it near your eyes.

PREP TIME: 10 TO 15 MINUTES

1 cup unsalted butter, softened

2 stalks lemongrass, trimmed and chopped

1$^1/_2$ tablespoons peeled and chopped fresh ginger

4 shallots, chopped

1 tablespoon good-quality dark soy sauce (preferably Japanese)

2 teaspoons sugar

$^1/_4$ teaspoon ground turmeric

$^1/_4$ teaspoon ground cumin

In a food processor fitted with a metal blade, combine all the ingredients and process until very smooth.

Transfer the mixture to a fine-mesh sieve and work it through the mesh with the back of a ladle. Discard whatever remains in the sieve.

Serving Suggestions

This is mainly a butter for adding authentic Asian flavor to your cooking. For a refreshing change from Western seafood dishes, try sautéing shrimp or briefly searing scallops on both sides in this butter.

Stir-fry strips of chicken, beef, or pork with the butter in a wok over a high flame and serve atop a bed of steamed white rice.

Excellent for stir-frying or sautéing any vegetable side dish to accompany Asian meals.

Sun-Dried Tomato Butter

Because the drying process concentrates the distinctive flavor and aroma of ripe tomatoes, this butter has a very intense taste. You can get sun-dried tomatoes in two forms: dry, usually in a plastic bag and requiring marinating, and packed in oil. I like to know exactly what's in all my food, so I prefer the dry kind. If you're the same, get the dry kind and rehydrate in any marinade you want.

PREP TIME: 30 TO 35 MINUTES

1 ounce sun-dried tomatoes

1 cup unsalted butter, softened

2 sprigs thyme, finely chopped

1 small clove garlic, crushed

Salt

If you are using dry-packed sun-dried tomatoes, soak them in 2 cups warm water and 2 tablespoons red wine vinegar for 15 minutes. Drain in a colander and gently press out excess liquid. If you are using oil-packed sun-dried tomatoes, drain them in a colander. (It's a good idea to reserve the flavorful oil for other uses later on.)

In a food processor fitted with a metal blade, combine the tomatoes, butter, thyme, garlic, and salt and process until smooth.

Serving Suggestions

This butter can enrich any sauce with its beautiful blend of butter, garlic, and thyme, but it's especially suited to finishing tomato sauces. Simply dice some of the prepared butter and slowly mix it into any of your pasta, poultry, fish, or meat sauces.

Refrigerate diced cubes of the butter and sprinkle them over your pizzas and lasagnas before baking to give these dishes extra smooth tomato flavor.

For a taste of an authentic Italian steak house, sear cuts of filet mignon on both sides, then dollop some of this butter on top and bake to your desired doneness. Serve dolloped with a bit more butter and crispy loaves of ciabatta to soak up every last savory drop of tomato-and-thyme-tinged steak juice.

Tarragon Butter

Tarragon's gentle aroma of anise and fresh green grass is a traditional favorite of the French. Its flavor is far more delicate than that of star anise, and so it is often used in dishes that require a subtle flavor of anise. You'll need fresh tarragon for this recipe, of course, so try to find it at the supermarket or your local fresh vegetable market. If you usually have trouble finding fresh tarragon, buy a lot when you do and just freeze it. Frozen tarragon is a great substitute for fresh, but dried should never be used.

PREP TIME: 10 MINUTES, PLUS 40 MINUTES
    CHILLING

4 to 5 sprigs tarragon

1 cup unsalted butter, softened

1 clove garlic, crushed

$1/2$ teaspoon salt

Separate the tarragon leaves from their stems and discard the stems. Using a very sharp knife, gently chop the tarragon, taking care not to overchop it or it will become limp.

In a mixing bowl, combine the butter, tarragon, garlic, and salt and mix well with a wooden spoon.

Roll the butter into a cylinder using waxed paper or plastic wrap. Refrigerate for at least 40 minutes before serving.

Serving Suggestions

To add mouth-watering flavor to roast chicken, preheat the oven to 350°F. Massage softened tarragon butter into the skin, then roast until the flesh is tender and the skin is crispy (about 20 minutes per pound).

For healthy, homemade pizzas that put commercial pies to shame, preheat the oven to 350°F. Roll out raw canned biscuit dough into individual pizzas, then stir-fry thinly sliced vegetables (such as red onion, peppers, zucchini, and eggplant) in a spoonful of tarragon butter. Top the dough with vegetables, sprinkle with coarse salt and freshly milled black pepper, and crumble on feta cheese or any other cheese you like. Dollop a bit of softened tarragon butter on top, then bake until golden brown, 5 to 7 minutes for soft and chewy or 10 to 12 minutes for crispy.

Tomato-Basil Butter

Caprese is a traditional Italian salad that consists of a simple combination of fresh, ripe tomatoes, basil leaves, and mozzarella cheese. This butter is as creamy and delicious as the traditional dish, but suitable for accenting everything from garlic bread to filet mignon. For an especially aromatic variation, you can mix freshly crushed garlic cloves into the butter just before rolling into a cylinder (see page 37).

PREP TIME: 15 TO 20 MINUTES, PLUS 40 MINUTES CHILLING

2 firm, ripe tomatoes (preferably plum tomatoes)

2 sprigs sweet basil

1 cup unsalted butter, softened

1/2 teaspoon salt

To facilitate peeling, place the tomatoes in a bowl and cover with boiling water. Let stand for 1 to 2 minutes, then drain, rinse in cold water, and peel. (The skins should now come off very easily.) Halve the peeled tomatoes, discard the seeds, and finely dice the flesh. Set aside.

Separate the basil leaves from their stems and discard the stems. With a very sharp knife, shred the basil into narrow strips, taking care not to put too much pressure on the knife, which causes the basil to brown very quickly.

In a bowl, combine the butter, tomatoes, basil, and salt and blend together with a wooden spoon just until combined. When you can clearly see that the tomatoes and basil are well distributed throughout the butter, stop mixing immediately, or the mixture will start to become an unattractive pink paste.

Taste and adjust the seasoning, then roll the butter into a cylinder with waxed paper or plastic wrap. Refrigerate for at least 40 minutes before serving.

Serving Suggestions

To give broiled fish a lovely, colorful shine, slice thick coins from the cylinder, rest atop the warm fish, and let melt.

Slightly melt 1 to 2 tablespoons of the butter and rub it onto steaks. Grill and serve with extra sliced coins and baked potatoes topped with a dollop of the softened butter.

Spicy Butters

Hot Chile and Garlic Butter

This piquant butter is the chile lover's dream spread. It contains a simple combination of finely diced hot chiles and freshly crushed garlic, giving it a lovely odor that complements its zing of hot flavor.

PREP TIME: 10 TO 15 MINUTES

3 fresh small hot chiles

1 cup unsalted butter, softened

3 cloves garlic, crushed

Generous pinch of salt

Cut the chiles lengthwise, remove and discard the seeds, then chop very small.

In a mixing bowl, combine the chiles, butter, garlic, and salt and blend with a wooden spoon until well combined. Taste and adjust the seasoning.

Serving Suggestions

Put a little fire under your guests' appetites: serve room-temperature this butter as a spicy dip with vegetables, minitoasts, crackers, or nachos. Spread on tortillas and tacos before filling with vegetables, meats, and cheeses.

Rub onto steaks or pork chops just before roasting. You can even sauté meats and vegetables in this butter and dollop the hot dish with it once more before serving.

Dollop onto seafood such as shrimp, scallops, or fish fillets and broil until tender.

Chipotle Pepper Butter

Chipotle peppers lend a unique, smoky flavor to dishes because they are jalapeño peppers that have been smoked over a wood fire. The smokiness—and fire—of the chipotle is an integral flavor in both Mexican and international cuisine. They are mostly found seasoned and marinated (often in adobo sauce) in cans, but you can find the dried peppers sold in cellophane bags. For spicy-food lovers who find butter's smooth flavor just too boring, this is the fiery dairy product for you.

PREP TIME: 10 TO 15 MINUTES

1 cup unsalted butter, softened

2 tablespoons canned chipotle peppers, undrained

2 tablespoons chopped shallot

1 tablespoon chopped fresh cilantro

1 clove garlic, crushed

1/4 teaspoon salt

In a food processor fitted with a metal blade, combine all the ingredients and process for about 5 minutes.

Transfer to a fine sieve and work the mixture through the mesh using the back of a ladle. Discard what remains in the sieve.

Serving Suggestions

Adds extra sharp Mexican flavor to burritos and tacos. Just spread on the tortilla or shell right before filling with your favorite vegetables, meats, and cheeses.

Dolloped on grilled meat and fish, chipotle pepper butter can replace—even outdo—all the other hot sauces you usually sprinkle on.

Try stuffing this butter into the cavity and under the skin of a whole chicken, then roast in an oven preheated to 350°F for about 20 minutes per pound, until crisp and tender.

Curry Butter

This butter lets you add a little flavor of India to just about any dish, without hunting down any special ethnic ingredients. Everything we use here can be found at your local super-market. In fact, the variety of curry powders now readily available might make you dizzy; just try a few of them until you hit upon a favorite.

PREP TIME: 15 TO 20 MINUTES

1 cup unsalted butter, softened

2 teaspoons good-quality curry powder

$1/2$ teaspoon sugar

$1/2$ teaspoon salt

1 teaspoon freshly squeezed lemon juice

4 shallots, finely diced

2 cloves garlic, crushed

2 teaspoons chopped fresh cilantro

In a mixing bowl, combine the butter, curry powder, sugar, salt, and lemon juice. With a wooden spoon, blend until the spices are evenly distributed and the sugar and salt have completely dissolved. Blend in the shallots, garlic, and cilantro. Taste and adjust the seasoning.

Serving Suggestions

For a positively unforgettable warm salmon salad, poach a salmon until just ready, then shred it into bite-sized pieces and toss with freshly chopped chile peppers, cilantro, and red onion. Dress with a little melted curry butter and red wine vinegar.

To give your lamb stew a little curry spice, start off by browning the cubes of meat in this butter.

Spread a thick layer onto floured lamb or pork chops, then roast in an oven preheated to 350°F for about 15 minutes, until tender.

Substitute curry butter for regular butter in your risottos and pilafs to create the perfect complement to any of the above main courses.

Dijon Mustard Butter

Dijon is the province in France that is known worldwide for its excellent mustard. Dijon mustards are produced in many countries, however, so try several and determine which one you like best, then use it in the following recipe. Dijon mustard contains less turmeric than other mustard spreads—the bright yellow color we associate with mustard is actually from the turmeric seasoning, not the mustard seeds themselves—so it is not as yellow as other varieties. If you'd like your Dijon butter to be bright yellow, you can always add a little more turmeric.

PREP TIME: 10 TO 15 MINUTES

1 cup unsalted butter, softened

1 tablespoon grainy Dijon mustard

1 tablespoon smooth Dijon mustard

1 tablespoon finely chopped shallot

1 tablespoon red wine vinegar

$1/2$ teaspoon salt

1 teaspoon sugar

1 teaspoon chopped fresh thyme

$1/4$ teaspoon ground turmeric

In a mixing bowl, combine all the ingredients and mix together with a wooden spoon until well blended. Taste the mixture and adjust the seasoning. You may want to add more sugar or salt; just remember that sugar will reduce acidic flavor, while salt will enhance it. Serve immediately or roll into a cylinder and refrigerate.

Serving Suggestions

Mustard butter melts very nicely on a hot dog or in mashed potatoes. Use it as a spread in beef or turkey sandwiches, or sauté strips of meat in the butter and serve on a bed of romaine lettuce (no dressing required!).

Paprika Butter

This is a nice, smooth butter that you can make either mild or fiery. The generous pinch of hot paprika is what adds the zest. You can, of course, be as generous as you like and add as much zest as suits your palate. Try not to overdo it, though, or you'll make your butter grainy. (And remember that the mustard also adds some bite.) The best paprika comes from Hungary, but Moroccan paprika is also highly regarded.

PREP TIME: 5 MINUTES

1/2 cup salted butter, softened

1 teaspoon good-quality Dijon mustard or any other French or Belgian mustard

1 tablespoon sweet paprika (preferably Hungarian or Moroccan)

Generous pinch hot paprika (optional)

Salt

Juice of 1/2 lemon

In a small bowl, whisk together the butter and mustard. Sprinkle in the paprikas and salt and blend well while gradually adding the lemon juice. Blend until well combined. Pipe rosettes onto a baking sheet and refrigerate or spread on waxed paper and roll into a cylinder, refrigerate, then unroll and slice. If you are using this as a spread, serve at room temperature.

Serving Suggestions

Use this piquant butter instead of plain butter to spice up sandwiches.

To enrich white-meat chicken, pork, veal, or turkey sauces with color and flavor, dice the cylindered butter and whisk it into the sauce at the last moment.

Serve with barbecued steaks, chops, and so on by slicing the cylindered butter and placing it atop the hot meat. Let melt and glaze, then serve immediately.

Paprika Butter (opposite page) and Lemon Butter (page 28)

Roasted Jalapeño Butter

The combination of roasted peppers, cilantro, cumin, and freshly crushed garlic works remarkably well. I prefer red jalapeños in this recipe because they tend to be somewhat sweeter than the green ones, and they give the butter a particularly bright, festive color. If you don't have a charcoal grill or a gas stove, you can roast the jalapeños in an oven preheated to 475°F (or just place them under the broiler) for 3 to 7 minutes. Check and turn them frequently.

PREP TIME: 20 MINUTES

2 fresh red or green jalapeños

1 cup unsalted butter, softened

2 cloves garlic, crushed

2 tablespoons chopped fresh cilantro

$1/4$ teaspoon ground cumin

Generous pinch of salt

Roast the jalapeños on a charcoal grill or over an open gas flame for 3 to 7 minutes on each side, until the skins are black and cracked, but the flesh is still firm to the touch. Place in a plastic bag and close tightly to enable the steam to soften the skins (this makes peeling the peppers much easier). Let cool in the bag.

When cool enough to handle, peel the jalapeños, slice them open, and remove and discard the seeds. Cut into thin strips.

In a mixing bowl, combine the jalapeños with the butter, garlic, cilantro, cumin, and salt. Blend with a wooden spoon. Taste and adjust the seasoning.

Serving Suggestions

You can roll the butter into cylinders and refrigerate them for later use or serve it immediately at room temperature as a spread. For a colorful and appetizing starter, dollop or spread onto minitoasts.

This butter is delicious served cool on barbecued meats with a side of fresh arugula leaves.

Incorporate into stews and soups by browning meats in the melted butter before adding vegetables and water.

Horseradish Butter

This butter is incredibly easy to make and yet bursts with distinctive flavor all the same. Be careful with peeled horseradish root until you get it into water: it is incredibly potent, so open a window, try not to touch it with bare hands, and don't rub your eyes. If you always hold it in place with a towel as you cut it, you'll never experience anything but warm appreciation for its delightful burn.

PREP TIME: 15 MINUTES

2 inches fresh horseradish root

1 cup unsalted butter, softened

2 teaspoons white wine vinegar

1 teaspoon sugar

$^1/_2$ teaspoon salt

Peel the horseradish and cut into rounds $^3/_8$ inch thick. Cover with cold water in a small bowl and soak for 5 minutes, then drain in a colander. (If you're a real fire eater, you can skip the soaking. It just cools things down.)

In a food processor fitted with a metal blade, combine the horseradish, butter, vinegar, sugar, and salt and process until very smooth.

Serving Suggestions

White-fleshed fish has never met a better friend than this butter. Dollop a teaspoon of softened butter on poached fish fillets or cover raw fillets with a few slices of refrigerated butter and broil until pale golden (5 to 7 minutes for a $^1/_2$-inch fillet; 12 to 15 minutes for a 2-inch fillet). Try with other seafood as well.

Traditionally an accent for meats, horseradish can be used to complement steak, lamb, or pork chops. Simply drop on a few dollops of this butter before or after cooking.

A wonderful spread in salami sandwiches, or with any other cold cuts, for that matter. Even fill a roll with flavor: bury a teaspoon of the butter in the center of a raw canned biscuit and bake as directed. As the dough heats up and spreads out, the butter will melt and saturate the entire bun.

Place a generous amount of horseradish butter atop a bed of warm, steamed white rice to add a little kick to an otherwise boring side dish.

Nut and Seed Butters

All-Natural Peanut Butter

Homemade peanut butter is easy to make and much better than the supermarket variety; all-natural ingredients mean all-natural flavor. Plus, you can adjust the recipe to the sweetness you desire, or leave out the sugar altogether.

Peanut skins contain valuable nutrients, but they add a slightly bitter aftertaste to the peanut butter. You can peel them if the taste bothers you, but peeling is time-consuming, so at least try the recipe with the skins on first. Do not be tempted to use commercially roasted peanuts, which are heavily salted and usually roasted in fat.

If you prefer, you can substitute any other vegetable oil for the peanut oil, though canola and soy oil don't give such good results. I suggest trying this recipe with dark sesame oil, which enhances the flavor of the roasted peanuts and adds a touch of sesame flavor that makes for an interesting change of pace from plain peanut butter.

PREP TIME: 30 MINUTES

1 cup raw peanuts

1 to 2 tablespoons peanut oil

1/2 teaspoon salt

3 to 4 tablespoons sugar (optional)

Preheat the oven to 300°F.

Place the peanuts on a cookie sheet and roast for 15 to 20 minutes, until golden brown. Remove from oven and let cool in the pan.

To peel, rub the cooled peanuts between your hands and discard the skins as they fall off.

Transfer the peanuts to a food processor fitted with a metal blade and process for a few minutes, until a very thick paste begins to form. Continuing to process without pause, begin adding the oil as slowly as possible by pouring a very thin stream through the feed tube. Add only as much oil as is necessary to obtain the consistency of peanut butter you prefer. Process just until well blended for chunky, a little longer for creamy; the longer you process, the closer the peanut butter will get to a thin paste (which is how you want it if you intend to cook with it).

Taste the peanut butter, add the salt and sugar, if you want to sweeten it, and process until dissolved.

Serving Suggestions

Spread with homemade strawberry jam on a warm piece of bread for a traditionally delicious, all-natural favorite you can enjoy any hour of the day.

Slightly soften 2 cups of vanilla ice cream at room temperature for 5 to 7 minutes, then process with 2 tablespoons salted, unsweetened peanut butter for 3 to 4 minutes. Return to the freezer for 2 hours, then enjoy the freshest, most superb peanut butter ice cream you've ever tasted.

Incorporate peanut butter into warm vanilla sauces for topping waffles or pancakes.

Knead plain cookie dough with 2 tablespoons peanut butter and bake as directed. You'll be surprised at how sensational such a simple treat can be.

This natural peanut butter is also perfect for thick Indonesian sauces and other Southeast Asian dishes. Just blend 1 to 2 tablespoons into any of your noodle, beef, pork, or chicken sauces for an amazing, authentic experience of the East.

Cashew Butter

The simple combination of roasted cashew nuts and butter is one of my favorites. In order to achieve the best possible result, try to find a very pure, high-quality butter, preferably a European one. Dutch, French, Belgian, and Irish butters are readily available in most supermarkets and have a naturally nutty flavor that blends beautifully with the cashews. You can buy roasted cashew nuts or roast fresh ones yourself.

The butter is best blended with a pestle and mortar. You can use your food processor, but be sure to process the butter and nuts together in short bursts so that you don't wind up with a smooth paste.

All nuts taste best fresh roasted, so you will notice a decline in flavor the longer you keep this butter. It is best to make it as close as possible to serving time.

PREP TIME: 15 TO 20 MINUTES

2 tablespoons roasted cashew nuts

1 cup unsalted butter, softened

Pinch of salt (optional)

In a mortar, roughly pound the nuts with a pestle to release their flavor. If you are using a food processor, coarsely chop the nuts.

Add the butter and pound together with the nuts just until combined. Or process until the nuts are finely chopped and evenly distributed throughout the butter.

Taste the cashew butter and adjust the seasoning, if necessary; roasted cashew nuts usually come salted.

Serving Suggestions

Try cashew butter in sandwiches with cold cuts or corned beef and green vegetables.

You can sear scallops in this butter. Preheat your skillet, melt the butter, drop in the scallops, and cook for $1^{1}/_{2}$ to 2 minutes on each side, until the flesh turns opaque but the centers are still translucent. Boil small new potatoes and coat them in it as well to serve as a side.

Hazelnut Butter

This is a nondairy spread that is nothing more than hazelnuts, oil, and two little extras that just round out its flavor. If you're making it for kids, diabetics, or anybody on a diet, feel free to reduce or completely eliminate the sugar. If you buy roasted nuts, be sure to get the unsalted variety. As with all nut butters, the amount of oil you'll need will depend upon the fat content in your particular batch of nuts.

PREP TIME: 30 MINUTES

1 cup hazelnuts

1 cup confectioner's sugar

Pinch of salt

1 to 3 tablespoons vegetable oil

Preheat the oven to 300°F.

Roast the hazelnuts on a cookie sheet for about 15 minutes, until golden in color. Remove from the oven, transfer to a cool baking pan, and let cool completely. If the slightly bitter taste of the skins bothers you, you can peel the cool hazelnuts by rubbing them between your hands and discarding the skins as they fall off.

In a food processor fitted with a metal blade, process the hazelnuts until a paste is formed. Add the sugar and salt and process for 4 more minutes.

Without pausing or stopping the processing, begin adding the vegetable oil by pouring it through the feed tube in a very thin stream. Add only the amount of oil needed to obtain a thick, smooth paste, exactly the consistency of peanut butter.

Transfer the butter to an airtight jar and store in a cool, dry place. Use within 2 weeks.

Serving Suggestions

You can substitute hazelnut butter anytime you would use regular peanut butter: in cookie doughs, ice cream, for ants-on-a-log, or as a spread on warm bread or rolls.

For a great natural, healthy snack you can keep in the refrigerator for unexpected company, melt 7 ounces bittersweet chocolate and mix with 2 tablespoons hazelnut butter and 3 cups cornflakes. Drop spoonfuls onto waxed paper and refrigerate for about 10 to 15 minutes, until firm.

Pecan Butter

You'll find this butter, which can be used in both sweet and savory dishes, quite versatile. The flavor of fresh chopped pecans adds a nutty, foresty flavor to the fresh creaminess of the butter. It's a good way to use up all those Southern pecans you bought in the fall, and it can be added to most any traditional pecan dessert to intensify its sweet Southern flavor.

PREP TIME: 15 MINUTES

2 tablespoons pecans

1 cup unsalted butter, softened

Pinch of salt

Preheat the oven to 350°F.

Roast the pecans on a cookie sheet for about 5 minutes, just until they begin to brown. Transfer immediately to a cool cookie sheet and let cool for 5 minutes.

Coarsely chop the nuts. In a mixing bowl, combine the nuts with the butter and salt. Use a wooden spoon to mix together until well blended.

Serving Suggestions

To give a little nutty crunch to tender seafood dishes, slightly melt 2 tablespoons of this butter and drizzle over 1 cup bread crumbs, mix together well, and sprinkle over raw fish fillets or scallops. Broil until the seafood is tender and the crumbs turn golden.

Pecan butter is wonderful sliced into thin coins and added to cheese or pastrami sandwiches.

Work 2 tablespoons of pecan butter into $1/4$ cup all-purpose flour, sprinkle over apple pies, and bake until golden brown.

Pistachio Butter

Simple yet rich in flavor and texture, this butter has endless culinary uses, both savory and sweet. A little interesting fact for you: it doesn't pay to force open a completely closed pistachio shell, because only the nuts that have grown enough to open the shell by themselves are actually edible. The nut inside of a closed shell isn't yet developed enough to eat and should be thrown away. I recommend you roast the pistachios yourself (you'll need to shell them first), but if you do buy them prepared, be absolutely sure to get an unsalted variety.

PREP TIME: 10 MINUTES

4 ounces unsalted shelled raw pistachios

1 cup unsalted butter, softened

Salt and freshly milled black pepper

Preheat the oven to 350°F.

Roast the pistachios on a cookie sheet for 5 to 7 minutes, until they're golden on the outside but still green on the inside.

In a food processor fitted with a metal blade, process the pistachios just until finely chopped—stop before they are ground into a powder. Add the butter and process just until well combined. Add the salt and pepper to taste, pulsing only very briefly to blend in.

Serving Suggestions

I use this butter quite a lot to finish sauces with a nice nutty flavor. Just whisk in 2 tablespoons of the butter for each 1 cup of sauce at the very last moment.

Substitute pistachio butter for the unflavored butter called for in your pastry recipes—the extra nutty flavor and little crunchy surprises in every bite make very interesting baked goods.

When making hollandaise sauce for a special dinner, try substituting pistachio butter for plain butter and serving over steamed asparagus or leeks.

Savory Pecan Butter

An interesting spin on traditional pecan butter. The soy sauce gives this version unusual zing, while the natural sweetness of honey enhances the subtle sweetness of the pecans.

PREP TIME: 20 TO 25 MINUTES

1 cup unsalted butter

1 cup pecans

1 tablespoon honey

1 teaspoon soy sauce

2 teaspoons salt

Preheat a large skillet over medium-low heat. Add the butter and pecans and cook, stirring occasionally, for 5 to 7 minutes, until the pecans are toasted and coated with butter. Remove from heat and let cool for 10 minutes in the skillet.

When the pecans are completely cool, transfer them to a food processor fitted with a metal blade. Add the honey, soy sauce, and salt and process until smooth.

Serving Suggestions

Use this butter spread any time you would use ordinary peanut butter: in sandwiches with jelly, for ants-on-a-log, or to turn simple peanut butter cookies into mouth-watering savory pecan butter cookies.

To thicken and enrich Asian dishes with a roast pecan flavor, toss noodles, stir-fry, or vegetables in 1 tablespoon of the softened spread.

Tired of the same old Southern pecan dishes? Spice things up a little by substituting savory pecan butter for regular butter and see what a little soy sauce can do for the South.

Pumpkin Seed Butter

The pumpkin seeds that you use for this butter should still have that lovely, nutty flavor of fresh, ripe pumpkin. The butter should also be high quality, very fresh, and rich in milky flavor. If you buy fresh, already hulled pumpkin seeds to roast at home, they should be a deep khaki green color and unsalted.

PREP TIME: 20 MINUTES

3 tablespoons hulled pumpkin seeds
1 cup unsalted butter, softened
Generous pinch of salt

Preheat the oven to 300°F.

Spread out the seeds in a single layer on a cookie sheet. Roast for 10 to 15 minutes, turning occasionally with a spatula. When the seeds are golden on the inside, transfer to a cool cookie sheet and let cool completely. The pumpkin seeds will become very crispy when cooled.

Divide the cooled seeds into two batches; finely chop one and coarsely chop the other.

In a mixing bowl, combine the butter, salt, and finely chopped seeds. Blend together well, using a wooden spoon. Add the coarsely chopped seeds and work them into the mixture until a thick-textured butter forms.

Serving Suggestions

Make your sandwiches a little "nutty" by spreading on a generous layer of pumpkin seed butter before adding cold cuts, cheeses, smoked fish, or egg salad.

The butter adds crunchy texture and smooth, earthy flavor to tender seafood. Sear scallops in melted pumpkin seed butter—just 1 minute on each side.

Remove cooked mussels from their shells, chop, mix with 1 tablespoon bread crumbs and plenty of pumpkin seed butter, and place a spoonful in each mussel shell. Place under the broiler for 1 to 2 minutes, until pale golden. Garnish with sprigs of parsley and serve immediately.

Fry any type of firm white-fleshed fish in pumpkin seed butter. The butter turns a lovely golden brown, and the pumpkin seeds crisp even more, adding color and texture to the fish.

Sesame Butter

This is an unexpected combination, but trust me, it's positively ingenious. The recipe demands almost no effort and yet produces amazing results. Dark sesame oil is available at larger supermarkets and Asian specialty shops.

PREP TIME: 10 MINUTES

2 tablespoons sesame seeds

1 cup unsalted butter, softened

2 tablespoons dark sesame oil

$^1/_2$ teaspoon salt

$^1/_2$ teaspoon sugar

In a frying pan over medium heat, toast the sesame seeds for 5 to 7 minutes, until they turn pale golden, stirring frequently to prevent overbrowning. Transfer the seeds to a bowl and let cool completely.

Add the butter, sesame oil, salt, and sugar to the bowl. Use a wooden spoon to mix all the ingredients together until well blended. Taste and adjust the seasoning.

Serving Suggestions

Spread this butter on warm toast and enjoy with soft-boiled eggs for breakfast.

Toss poached green vegetables, such as Brussels sprouts, broccoli, or green beans, with sesame butter and serve as a side dish to steak.

Sauté a handful or two of spinach in this melted butter and serve atop macaroni and cheese.

Substitute sesame butter for the regular butter in your cookie dough recipes. (Just omit the salt from the original recipe, because the butter already contains it.)

Seafood Butters

Anchovy Butter

Even if you don't like anchovies on your pizza, you probably love them in a Caesar salad, so go ahead and at least try them in butter. Most people who say they don't like anchovies have only ever eaten stale ones; they are very perishable and need to be used up within a couple of days. There are ways to preserve them for longer, but it's best just to open a fresh can or jar for this recipe. This is a very salty, strongly flavored butter that's excellent all by itself as a spread or in sandwiches.

PREP TIME: 5 MINUTES

3 ounces oil-packed anchovy fillets (preferably Italian or Greek)

1 cup unsalted butter, softened

Freshly milled black pepper

1 teaspoon good-quality red wine vinegar

Drain the anchovy fillets. In a food processor fitted with a metal blade, combine the anchovies, butter, and black pepper and process until a smooth paste forms. Add the vinegar and continue to process until well blended.

Serving Suggestions

Anchovy butter is wonderful all by itself on warm toast.

Pour slightly melted anchovy butter on bread cubes and bake at 350°F for 5 to 7 minutes, until golden brown. Use as richly flavored croutons for Caesar salad.

Great for finishing fish and seafood sauces, enriching them with a salty, nutty flavor. When using in sauces, though, season sparingly; the butter itself is quite salty.

Asian Shrimp Butter

You can avoid the dull brown color that soy sauce gives to butter by using a light-colored soy sauce, available at Chinese and most other Asian grocers. You can also substitute fish sauce (nam pla in Thai) for the soy sauce to enhance the natural flavor of the shrimp.

PREP TIME: 25 MINUTES, PLUS 30 MINUTES
    CHILLING

1 cup unsalted butter, slightly softened

4 ounces shrimp, peeled and deveined

2 cloves garlic, finely sliced

2 stalks lemongrass, trimmed and finely chopped

1 tablespoon light soy sauce

$1/2$ teaspoon sweet paprika

$1/2$ teaspoon sugar

Salt and freshly milled black pepper

In a frying pan over medium heat, melt $1^1/2$ tablespoons butter, taking care not to let it brown. Add the shrimp and garlic and sauté for 1 minute. Add the lemongrass and sauté for 1 more minute. Do not overcook the shrimp; they are ready when they turn a deep pink or vermillion red and are firm to the touch. (Overcooked shrimp will produce a grainy, not a smooth, butter.) As soon as they are cooked, transfer immediately to a separate bowl and set aside to cool completely.

In a food processor fitted with a metal blade, combine the remaining butter with the shrimp, soy sauce, paprika, and sugar. Process for a few minutes, until a thick but well-combined paste is formed. Pause the processing to taste and season with salt and pepper. Both the soy and fish sauces are very salty, so take care not to overseason.

Press the butter through a fine-mesh sieve. Discard what remains in the sieve.

Wrap in plastic wrap and roll into a cylinder. Refrigerate for at least 30 minutes.

Serving Suggestions

Dollop onto hot, freshly poached fish and let melt. Or cut into small cubes and toss with warm noodles and seafood to enrich the seafood flavor of the dish. Try dolloping the butter on opened clams, oysters, or mussels and broil briefly, or sautéing seafood in a frying pan or wok.

Lobster Butter

Lobster butter is not something you prepare every day. Make it just for special occasions or to add to gourmet dishes, because it will take some time and effort. Though frozen lobster meat might usually taste pretty good, you'll need the lobster shells as well for this recipe, so fresh ones are the only way to go. If you can't find fresh, go ahead and use frozen, but discard the shells once you've extracted the meat.

PREP TIME: 4 TO 5 HOURS

2 (25- to 28-ounce) lobsters

1³/₄ cups plus 2 tablespoons unsalted butter

2 ribs celery, chopped

1 onion, chopped

1 carrot, chopped

2 tablespoons cognac or brandy

3 tablespoons tomato paste

1 clove garlic, crushed

1 sprig fresh thyme

1 sprig fresh tarragon

5 whole peppercorns

1 bay leaf (fresh or dried)

Bring a large pot of salt water to a boil, drop in the lobsters, and boil for 8 to 10 minutes, until just cooked through. Drain and then submerge in cold water for 2 to 3 minutes, or until cool enough to handle. Shell the lobsters, taking care to extract as much flesh as possible. Set both the shells and the meat aside. (Discard the shells if you used frozen lobsters.)

In a large saucepan over medium-low heat, melt 2 tablespoons of the butter. Add the celery, onion, and carrot and sauté for a few minutes, just until translucent. Add the cognac and simmer for 3 to 4 minutes over high heat, until all the alcohol has evaporated.

Add the lobster meat, shells, remaining 1³/₄ cups butter, tomato paste, garlic, thyme, tarragon, peppercorns, and bay leaf. Decrease the heat to as low as possible and simmer very gently for 3 hours, scraping off any foam that rises to the surface with a slotted spoon.

Strain the liquid through a fine-mesh sieve. Firmly press the solids that remain in the sieve against the mesh in order to extract as much liquid and flavor as possible. Discard the solids that remain in the sieve and set the liquid aside to cool at room temperature for 10 to 20 minutes.

Strain the liquid again (ideally through several layers of cheesecloth), leaving any milky residue on the bottom of the saucepan. Transfer the butter to an airtight container and refrigerate up to 1 week. Serve melted.

Serving Suggestions

The recipe makes an especially large amount of butter so that you can enjoy it as often as possible even without making it every day. To store it, pour the liquid butter into an ice cube tray and freeze, then just defrost the right amount whenever you need it for cooking.

Obviously, this is the perfect butter for sautéing lobster, shrimp, squid, and scallops. Just heat 1 tablespoon lobster butter over high heat and sauté the seafood until tender, then pour over 1 tablespoon cognac and season with a little salt and pepper. Sprinkle with chopped parsley and serve.

I make a gorgeous lobster hollandaise with this butter. All you have to do is replace the regular butter in your favorite hollandaise recipe with lobster butter, then serve poured over cooked lobsters and freshly poached asparagus.

Any time you make a fish or seafood sauce, finish it by whisking in 1 to 2 tablespoons of this butter. Try finishing a seafood risotto the same way.

Crabmeat Butter Dip

This recipe is so easy to make yet so incredibly rich that, while writing this book, I found myself constantly making batch after batch so I could keep pigging out on it. You don't even need to buy fresh crabs and extract the meat; just get the ready-made stuff from the supermarket freezer, defrost it, and toss it in. It's just as good in this recipe, so skip the hard work and spend all your time indulging. Don't be tempted to use a food processor, though; it makes the dip too runny.

PREP TIME: 5 MINUTES, PLUS 2 HOURS
    CHILLING

1/2 cup unsalted butter, softened

8 ounces cooked crabmeat

8 ounces cream cheese, softened

3 tablespoons mayonnaise

2 teaspoons freshly squeezed lemon juice

2 teaspoons Worcestershire sauce

1 small onion, diced

2 garlic cloves, crushed

Generous pinch of salt

Cocktail sauce, for serving

In a mixing bowl, combine the butter, crabmeat, cream cheese, mayonnaise, lemon juice, Worcestershire sauce, onion, garlic, and salt. Gently mix with a wooden spoon until well combined. Taste and adjust the seasoning. Transfer to a serving dish, cover with plastic wrap, and refrigerate for at least 2 hours to let the dip set.

Just before serving, remove the plastic wrap and cover the dip with a thin layer of cocktail sauce.

Serving Suggestions

Serve with lots of vegetables, minitoasts, nachos, crackers—anything!

Shrimp Butter

Bring a little flavor of French cuisine into your kitchen with this rich, smooth seafood butter. You can use any shrimp or prawns you like, but fresh will obviously give the best result.

PREP TIME: 25 TO 30 MINUTES

1 cup unsalted butter, softened

8 ounces shrimp or prawns, peeled and deveined

5 shallots, roughly chopped

2 cloves garlic, crushed

$1/2$ teaspoon salt

$1/8$ teaspoon freshly milled black pepper

2 tablespoons good-quality brandy (preferably cognac)

Pinch of sugar

1 tablespoon chopped fresh parsley (optional)

In a skillet over medium heat, melt 1 tablespoon butter. Add the shrimp and shallots and sauté for 3 to 5 minutes, until the shrimp are very pink and opaque and the shallots have turned translucent. Add the garlic, salt, and pepper and sauté for 1 more minute.

Pour in the brandy, increase the heat to high, and boil until all the alcohol evaporates.

Transfer the mixture to a food processor fitted with a metal blade. Add the sugar and let cool completely. (If the mixture is even slightly warm when you begin processing, your butter will turn out watery, so be patient.)

Process the cooled mixture until very smooth. Add the remaining butter and process for 5 minutes.

Transfer the butter to a fine-mesh sieve and work it through with the back of a ladle. Discard what remains in the sieve. Use a wooden spoon to mix the parsley into the butter for color.

Serving Suggestions

Sautéing any sort of shellfish in this butter considerably enhances its seafood flavor.

Try pouring melted shrimp butter over fresh bread cubes and baking at 350°F for 5 to 7 minutes, until crisp and golden. Use as croutons in all your green and seafood salads or just as a snack.

In a food processor fitted with a metal blade, process 1 cup bread crumbs and 1 tablespoon of this butter for 2 minutes. Dollop onto opened mussels, clams, or oysters, broil briefly, and serve warm. Or sprinkle the mixture over fish and bake.

Smoked Salmon Butter

Now that salmon is raised on farms, it is no longer a luxury food. If you can get your hands on it, though, you should try wild salmon at least once; it is much more tender, is finer in texture, and has a far richer seafood flavor than its domestically bred cousin. A very pink salmon will produce a handsome, deep pink spread, which you can enhance even further with a bit of paprika.

PREP TIME: 10 TO 15 MINUTES

1 cup unsalted butter, softened

4 ounces sliced smoked salmon

1 tablespoon cream cheese

$1/2$ teaspoon salt

1 teaspoon chopped flat-leaf parsley or dill (optional)

$1/4$ teaspoon good-quality sweet paprika

In a food processor fitted with a metal blade, process the butter and salmon together for 3 to 4 minutes, until completely smooth. Add the cream cheese and salt and process for 2 more minutes.

Taste and adjust the seasoning. If you are using parsley, add it now and process for a few more seconds, just until it's distributed throughout the butter. Stop immediately when you see that the herbs are worked through the spread, or it will begin to take on a dull olive green color.

To enhance that pink tint, you can process the ready spread with the paprika at any time.

Serving Suggestions

Smoked salmon butter is just heavenly on a warm bagel, with or without extra cream cheese and lox.

The next time you have white-fleshed fish for dinner, melt this spread slowly over low heat (overheating will cause it to curdle, so pay attention), then pour it over the baked or poached fish. The fish takes on a coppery, pink-orange color and an amazing richness of flavor.

Use a spatula to fill a pastry bag with the softened butter, attach a star-shaped nozzle to the bag, and pipe onto little sesame crackers to serve as an appetizer.

Pipe onto mini toasts and top with a quarter of a soft-boiled quail egg and red salmon caviar.

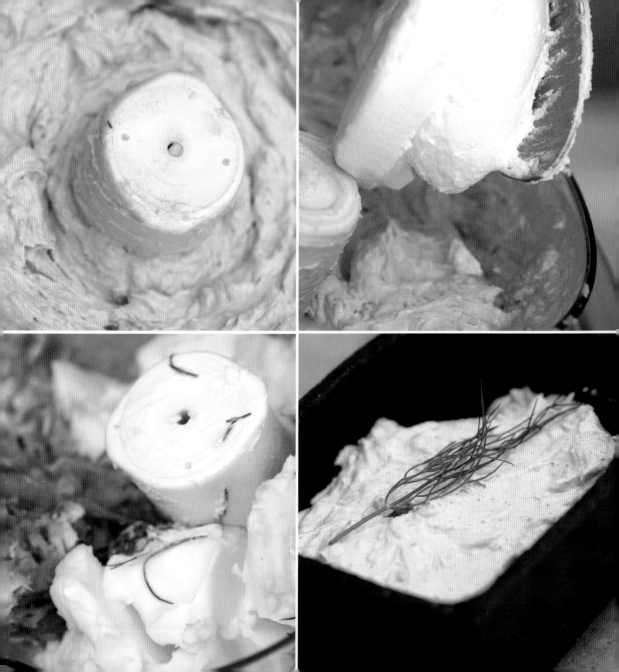

Sardine Sandwich Butter

These days you can find an abundance of high-quality sardines almost anywhere in the world. There are many ways to preserve and can sardines, but only one big distinction: some are cooked and packed in oil, while others are left uncooked and simply preserved in the can by salting. This latter variety has a fine, melt-in-your-mouth texture—clearly the best choice for a sardine butter. Greek and Italian ones are the very best because they are never exposed to any heat at all and so retain their richness and natural seafood flavor far better than others. If you can't find Greek or Italian, though, just use the best quality you can find. If you're in a hurry, buy the cooked ones, because the salted ones need to marinate for an hour.

PREP TIME: 10 TO 15 MINUTES

3 3/4 ounces canned sardines

1 cup unsalted butter, softened

Freshly milled black pepper

If you are using uncooked, salted sardines, remove them from the can and brush off any salt that clings to them. Marinate in olive oil for 1 hour, then drain off excess oil by placing them in a colander for a few minutes. For oil-packed sardines, simply drain them for a few minutes in a colander. Finely chop the drained sardines. There's no need to remove the heads or tails. They just add more flavor.

Transfer the sardines to a bowl, add the softened butter, and blend together well with a wooden spoon. The mixture should become somewhat pasty.

Taste and season with black pepper; 1/4 to 1/2 teaspoon is good, but I'm very generous with the pepper.

Serving Suggestions

Sardine butter is terrific spread in sandwiches that contain peppery green vegetables, such as arugula or watercress. It is ideal taken on a picnic, along with fresh, country-style bread and homemade salads and relishes.

Sweet Butters
and Buttercreams

Chocolate Buttercream

Because buttercreams require the addition of sugar for proper beating, I recommend using semisweet chocolate so that this buttercream doesn't come out too sweet. Fine chocolates have a very high cocoa solids content, which will produce a divinely rich chocolate flavor.

Always pay close attention when melting chocolate. You can either use a double boiler or a microwave set to low heat. Either way, do not overheat the chocolate, which causes the cocoa solids and the cocoa butter to separate, leaving you with grainy chocolate.

PREP TIME: 30 MINUTES

8 ounces high-quality semisweet chocolate

1 cup unsalted butter, softened

1/2 cup confectioner's sugar

Melt the chocolate in a double boiler or in a microwave oven. Set aside and allow to come to room temperature.

In the bowl of a standing electric mixer, beat the butter and confectioner's sugar on medium speed about 5 minutes, until pale and fluffy.

Reduce the speed to low and begin adding the cooled chocolate in a thin, steady stream, pausing from time to time to scrape the sides of the bowl to ensure thorough, even blending.

Increase the speed to medium and beat for 10 more minutes. The mixture should double in volume.

Variations: You can flavor your chocolate buttercream in an infinite variety of ways. Just add the extra ingredient during the last 10 minutes of beating. Start with one of these variations, which I find work beautifully with this buttercream in particular: grated zest of 1/2 orange, 2 teaspoons high-quality dark or white rum, 1 teaspoon good-quality instant coffee dissolved in 1 tablespoon water, or 1 tablespoon brandy or whiskey.

Serving Suggestions

This buttercream looks lovely (and tastes incredible) as a filling, icing, or decoration on cakes. Try spreading it between homemade ginger cookies or thin wafers to make a batch of delicious little cookie sandwiches.

Cinnamon-Honey Buttercream

There are all kinds of honey, and you'll find that each variety will give you quite a different butter. Try experimenting with them all until you find a favorite. Because honey thickens considerably when chilled, this butter tastes best at room temperature.

PREP TIME: 15 MINUTES, PLUS 15 TO 30
   MINUTES CHILLING

1 cup unsalted butter, softened

1/2 cup firmly packed light brown sugar

Pinch of salt

1/2 cup honey

2 cinnamon sticks, freshly ground

1 teaspoon good-quality vanilla extract

Grated zest of 1 orange (optional)

Using either a standing or hand-held mixer, beat the butter for about 5 minutes, until pale and fluffy. Add the brown sugar and salt and continue beating for 10 to 15 minutes, until the mixture is approximately twice its original volume.

Add the honey, cinnamon, vanilla, and orange zest a little bit at a time while continuing to beat, making sure each addition is well incorporated before adding the next. When all the ingredients are thoroughly blended, you should have a beige cream.

Transfer to a glass or ceramic bowl and refrigerate for at least 15 to 30 minutes, until the butter stiffens to about the consistency of a thick mayonnaise.

Serving Suggestions

Use as a filling or topping for caramel cakes, coffeecakes, and mini-éclairs. It makes a delicious spread on warm yeast pastries.

Coffee Buttercream

I use Italian brands of coffee for this recipe, but use any high-quality coffee for a fine result. As for the espresso, if you don't have a fancy coffee machine, better get the real thing from a nearby café.

PREP TIME: 25 TO 30 MINUTES

1 cup unsalted butter, softened

1 teaspoon fine coffee grounds

1 cup firmly packed light brown sugar

Pinch of salt

$1/4$ cup strong espresso or 2 teaspoons instant coffee dissolved in $1/4$ cup warm water, cooled to room temperature

1 teaspoon good-quality vanilla extract

In the bowl of a standing electric mixer, beat the butter, coffee grounds, brown sugar, and salt on low speed for 10 minutes.

Increase the speed to medium and very slowly add the espresso, pouring it in a thin, steady stream.

When all the espresso is incorporated, add the vanilla, scrape the sides of the bowl, and beat at medium speed for about 10 more minutes, until very fluffy. The buttercream should double in volume.

Serving Suggestions

Spread onto toast and nibble with your afternoon coffee. Fill, top, and decorate cakes, cupcakes, and other baked goods. Melt over your warm morning pancakes, waffles, and muffins.

Spread between two vanilla cookies, coffee buttercream beats any store-bought sandwich cookie filling.

Cranberry-Orange Butter

This sweet, colorful butter is sure to catch the eye—a perfect addition to cocktail or dinner parties. If you can't find candied cranberries, don't attempt to use plain dried ones; they are far too acidic for this recipe. Simply substitute candied cherries.

PREP TIME: 10 MINUTES

1 cup unsalted butter, softened

¹/₄ cup candied cranberries, finely chopped

Grated zest of 1 orange

¹/₂ cup confectioner's sugar

Pinch of salt (optional)

In a mixing bowl, combine the butter, cranberries, orange zest, and confectioner's sugar. Blend together well, using a wooden spoon. Taste the butter; you might want to add a pinch of salt to smoothen and enhance the blend of flavors.

Serving Suggestions

For a colorful, fruity dessert, halve and pit peaches or apricots, dollop a spoonful of cranberry-orange butter on each half, sprinkle with golden brown sugar, and place under the broiler for just a few minutes.

Serve warm with vanilla ice cream.

To give yeast pastries a little fruity accent, replace the regular butter called for by the recipe with this butter.

Hazelnut-Date Butter

This sweet butter can be used just as you would a buttercream. Real buttercreams take a little effort to make, though, while this simple butter requires no beating and no time-consuming process. Supermarkets carry a wide variety of dates, but soft-textured ones, such as Medjool dates, are recommended for this recipe. If you can't find Medjools or another soft-textured date, simply process any other kind for an extra one or two minutes in the food processor.

PREP TIME: 15 MINUTES

2 tablespoons raw unsalted hazelnuts

$1/2$ cup Medjool dates, pitted

3 to 4 tablespoons water

1 cup unsalted butter, softened

1 to 2 tablespoons confectioner's sugar (optional)

Preheat the oven to 350°F.

Roast the hazelnuts on a cookie sheet for 5 to 7 minutes, until pale golden on the inside. Set aside to cool on the sheet.

In a food processor fitted with a metal blade, process the dates and 3 tablespoons water for a few minutes, until a smooth paste forms. If you need to add more water to achieve a smooth paste, add it 1 tablespoon at a time. Be careful to stop when you have the consistency of paste so that the butter doesn't become too runny.

Coarsely chop the hazelnuts. (Don't bother to peel them; the skins add a nice texture to the butter.)

In a bowl, mix the butter, date paste, and chopped hazelnuts with a wooden spoon until well blended.

Taste the butter for sweetness. If you want it a little sweeter, mix in the confectioner's sugar with the wooden spoon.

Serving Suggestions

This butter is great on fresh, warm homemade muffins, morning toast, pancakes, waffles, and especially dessert crêpes.

For a delicious and unusual Middle Eastern treat, roll out ready-made puff pastry to a thickness of $1/8$ inch, spread on a layer of the butter, roll out again, and cut into strips. Place on a greased cookie sheet and bake in an oven preheated to 475°F for 5 to 7 minutes, until golden.

Maple Butter

Needless to say, good-quality, pure maple syrup is very important to this recipe. The popular brand that you put on your pancakes is probably not pure maple syrup, so check it and make sure you've got the right stuff. I expect you'll need to go buy a natural syrup, which is milder in flavor than the stuff intended only for pancakes. Maple extract is what helps fill out the flavor; you can find it at most any large supermarket.

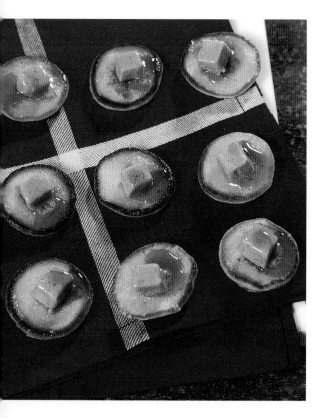

PREP TIME: 10 TO 15 MINUTES

1 cup salted butter, softened

1 cup confectioner's sugar

1/4 cup pure maple syrup

1 teaspoon maple extract

In a large bowl, beat together the butter and confectioner's sugar with a wooden spoon until smooth and somewhat fluffy.

Begin adding the maple syrup a little bit at a time, beating well after each addition. When all the syrup is well incorporated, add the maple extract and stir in thoroughly.

Serving Suggestions

Maple butter can be served chilled, at room temperature, or melted onto pancakes. Drizzle with some more maple syrup and serve. I like to refrigerate this butter, dice it, and place the cubes on silver dollar pancakes as a sweet treat at dinner parties. Top warm muffins with softened maple butter and enjoy with your morning coffee.

Marzipan-Honey Buttercream

This fine spread resembles the almond cream that the French use for filling and icing cakes. Use this butter to surprise your friends and family with gourmet desserts—you'll be surprised at just how easy it is. Compared to other buttercream recipes, this one calls for very little butter, so the beating time is especially short; and for a marzipan, it doesn't take nearly as much effort as the classic French one, yet is just as delicious.

PREP TIME: 15 TO 20 MINUTES

2 heaping tablespoons plain marzipan or almond paste

$1/2$ cup honey

1 teaspoon grated lemon zest

2 teaspoons almond liqueur (preferably Italian)

$1/4$ cup salted butter

Beat the marzipan and honey in the bowl of a standing electric mixer until a softened paste is formed. Add the lemon zest and liqueur and beat for 2 more minutes. Add the butter and beat for approximately 10 more minutes, until the mixture becomes slightly fluffy.

Serving Suggestions

This butter is best served at room temperature, spread on toast or muffins.

Because this fine-textured buttercream is so rich in flavor and texture but contains only a small amount of butter, it is especially suited for filling cakes, pies, and pastries before baking.

Roll out some ready-made puff pastry, spread with a thick layer ($1/2$ inch) of buttercream, top with thinly sliced apricots, apples, peaches, or pears, and bake in an oven preheated to 400°F for 7 to 10 minutes, until crisp and golden. Serve warm.

Milk and Honey Buttercream

A little attention is needed during the preparation of this sweet, smooth buttercream, but the result is definitely worth it. The darker the honey you use, the darker the buttercream. Just choose the honey you prefer; you won't care a bit about the color anyway once you've tasted it.

PREP TIME: 25 MINUTES

1 tablespoon honey

2 tablespoons water

$1/3$ cup condensed milk

1 cup unsalted butter, softened

$1/2$ cup confectioner's sugar

In a small heavy saucepan over medium heat, bring the honey to a boil. Simmer for about 4 minutes, or until honey becomes slightly darker. (Some honey varieties darken more quickly than others. Just be careful not to let yours burn. This procedure enhances the honey flavor in the buttercream.)

Once the honey has darkened slightly, remove it immediately from heat and pour in the water, whisking vigorously to form a syrup.

Using a scraper or a rubber spatula, transfer all the syrup to the bowl of a standing electric mixer fitted with the whisk attachment.

Stir in the condensed milk and whisk well. Let cool for about 10 minutes.

Add the butter and confectioner's sugar and beat on low speed for 5 minutes, pausing to scrape the sides of the bowl from time to time to ensure even blending. Once you have a smooth mixture, increase speed to medium and beat for 10 more minutes.

Serving Suggestions

The honey flavor of this butter makes it an ideal complement to all sorts of spiced cakes. Spread it on any—or all—of your special Christmas treats, from gingerbread cookies to German stollen.

Top or fill your fruitcakes, cinnamon rolls, and apple pies with this butter. It is wonderful spread on warm toast.

Peach and Ginger Buttercream

Peaches are often used whole in pastries for their gorgeous color, wonderful aroma, and juicy, sweet flavor. You can add that same lovely peachiness to other baked goods with peach butter. For this recipe, you should choose peaches that are very ripe but still firm to the touch, with no stains, cuts, or brown bruises. Use a vegetable peeler to gently slice off the skin, which should come off of ripe peaches quite easily. If you're a nectarine lover, try this recipe with them as well.

PREP TIME: 30 MINUTES

1 cup unsalted yellow butter, softened

¹/₂ cup confectioner's sugar

2 yellow peaches, peeled and minced

**1 teaspoon finely grated fresh ginger
     or crystallized ginger**

2 teaspoons bourbon

Pinch of salt

In the bowl of a standing electric mixer, beat the butter and confectioner's sugar for about 10 minutes, until pale and fluffy. Scrape the sides of the bowl frequently to ensure even blending.

Use the back of a ladle to work the minced peaches through a fine-mesh sieve into a small bowl. After the butter has turned pale and fluffy, begin adding the strained peaches to the mixture 1 tablespoon at a time, beating well after each addition and making sure that it is completely incorporated before adding the next.

Add the ginger, bourbon, and salt and beat for 10 more minutes, until the mixture has doubled in volume.

Serving Suggestions

Soak sponge cakes in a syrup consisting of 1 cup sugar and 1 cup water plus 2 tablespoons rum, then coat lightly with this buttercream. Refrigerate for at least 2 hours. Remove from refrigerator 10 to 15 minutes before serving.

Dollop on traditional Scottish shortbread or cupcakes.

Fill roulades with this cream for a fruity, mouth-watering dessert that is perfect for parties, picnics, holidays, and all sorts of celebrations.

Rich Buttercream

This buttercream is made with condensed milk, which enriches and intensifies the natural milk and butter flavors.

PREP TIME: 20 MINUTES

1 cup unsalted butter, softened

$1/2$ cup confectioner's sugar

$1/2$ cup condensed milk

Pinch of salt

In the bowl of a standing electric mixer, beat the butter and confectioner's sugar for 2 to 3 minutes at low speed, scraping the sides of the bowl from time to time to ensure that all the sugar is blended in.

Increase the speed to medium and beat for about 10 more minutes, until very pale and fluffy. Begin adding the condensed milk in a thin, steady stream, beating continuously until all is well incorporated. Add the salt and beat for another 10 minutes, until a pale, light, fluffy, rich-flavored buttercream forms.

Serving Suggestions

This buttercream is the perfect complement to scones, accompanied by fine tea. Fill cornmeal scones with homemade strawberry jam and top with this cream or spread or dollop on biscotti and serve with coffee.

Try on all your morning breads and pastries: toast, blueberry muffins, English muffins, bagels, and cinnamon rolls.

Dollop the buttercream onto hot fruit pies fresh out of the oven, spread it between madeleines to make sweet little sandwiches, fill cakes, and ice cupcakes with it.

Vanilla-Rum Buttercream

Didn't think your chocolate cake experience could get any better? Think again.

PREP TIME: 25 MINUTES

1 cup unsalted pale butter, softened

1 cup confectioner's sugar

1/2 vanilla pod, split lengthwise

Pinch of salt

2 tablespoons good-quality white rum

In the bowl of a standing electric mixer, beat the butter on medium speed for about 5 minutes, until fluffy and almost white in color.

Reduce the speed to low and add the confectioner's sugar. Beat just until combined, scraping the sides of the bowl from time to time to ensure thorough blending.

Using the tip of a sharp knife, scrape the black seeds from the split vanilla pod straight into the butter mixture. Beat on medium speed for at least 20 minutes. The mixture should increase in volume and become a fluffy, vanilla-scented cream, beautifully dotted with tiny black spots of vanilla.

Add the salt and continue beating at medium speed. Begin adding the rum a drop at a time.

(This will prevent the mixture from curdling and will help dissolve the remaining sugar.) Once all of the rum is well incorporated, beat for 5 more minutes.

Serving Suggestions

This buttercream is not just for icing. Spread it between cake layers, use it to fill roulades, and pipe it onto (or into) your pastries. Once you've tasted it, you'll never lack for ideas to use it.

Butter Sauces

Beurre Noisette
(Browned Butter Sauce)

This classic sauce is simple, yet incredibly versatile and tasty. The French name means "hazelnut butter," because browned butter releases wonderful nutty aromas reminiscent of roasted hazelnuts. To make the British version of beurre noisette, just omit the lemon.

PREP TIME: 5 MINUTES

1 cup salted butter

2 teaspoons freshly squeezed lemon juice

In a shallow saucepan over medium heat, melt the butter and continue to cook for several minutes, stirring constantly. The butter should begin to emit a distinctively nutty aroma as it begins to brown.

When it has turned deep golden, remove the butter from the heat and whisk in the lemon juice. Serve at once.

Serving Suggestions

This butter sauce is a particularly wonderful accompaniment to steamed sole, but try pouring it over any poached white-fleshed fish and sprinkling with toasted almond flakes.

Add a little gourmet class to fast food by pouring this sauce over crispy, golden french fries.

It is delicious, of course, poured over any type of meat. Try it on steaks, thin slices of roast beef, veal, pork chops, and even poultry.

Bread Crumb and Butter Sauce

Light and fresh, this super-easy sauce is endlessly versatile and will doubtless have you experimenting with all sorts of combinations in no time. The bread crumbs stay nice and crunchy so long as you serve the sauce immediately.

PREP TIME: 10 TO 15 MINUTES

1/2 cup unsalted butter

1 tablespoon diced red onion

3 tablespoons fresh or dried bread crumbs

1 hard-boiled egg, finely chopped or grated

1 teaspoon freshly squeezed lemon juice

2 tablespoons chopped fresh parsley

Generous pinch of salt

Freshly milled black pepper

In a saucepan over medium-low heat, melt the butter. Add the onion and sauté for 2 to 3 minutes, until translucent. Increase the heat to medium, add the bread crumbs, and sauté for 5 to 7 minutes, until golden.

Remove the saucepan from the heat and mix in the egg, lemon juice, parsley, salt, and pepper. Taste and adjust the seasoning. Serve right away (or those crunchy little crumbs will turn totally soggy).

Serving Suggestions

Serve over poached green vegetables such as broccoli, spinach, or green beans.

For a refreshing, light, Mediterranean side dish that's a perfect accompaniment to barbecued meats, fry thick slices of eggplant in oil, drizzle with some red wine vinegar, and top with this sauce.

Deep-fried slices of zucchini topped with yogurt and spoonfuls of this sauce make an exotic, delectable antipasti.

Hard-boil, peel, and halve a batch of eggs, then top with a spoonful of this sauce for a simple but filling appetizer that you might turn into a meal.

Cajun-Style Butter Sauce

Bring the flavors of New Orleans dancing onto your dinner table with this spicy butter sauce. There's more than one type of Cajun seasoning blend and hot sauce, so choose your favorite. Which stock you use, of course, depends on what you intend to serve the sauce with: use fish stock for seafood, chicken for poultry dishes, and veal for red meats.

PREP TIME: 15 MINUTES

¹⁄₂ cup cold unsalted butter, diced

1 tablespoon finely chopped shallot

¹⁄₂ teaspoon all-purpose flour

¹⁄₂ cup stock

2 teaspoons Cajun seasoning blend

1 teaspoon hot sauce

1 teaspoon Worcestershire sauce

¹⁄₄ teaspoon freshly squeezed lemon juice

In a saucepan over medium heat, melt 2 teaspoons of the butter. Add the shallot and sauté for about 3 minutes, until translucent. Add the flour and stir continuously for about 5 minutes, until it turns golden. Add the stock, Cajun seasoning, hot sauce, Worcestershire, and lemon juice. Increase the heat to high and bring to a boil. Decrease the heat to medium and simmer for 2 minutes, whisking from time to time to prevent lumps from forming. The sauce should thicken slightly.

Reduce heat to very low and begin whisking in the remaining butter a little bit at a time, making sure after each addition that it is well incorporated before adding the next. The sauce should thicken even more; it's ready when all the butter is blended in.

Serve immediately.

Serving Suggestions

This sauce is especially tasty with poached seafood. Dip cooked crab, lobster, scallops, shrimp, mussels, or squid in the sauce.

Obviously, it is delicious on traditional Cajun dishes, such as fried alligator nuggets and grilled catfish.

Prepared with chicken stock, the sauce brings out the cluck in a crispy roast chicken or braised turkey.

Make this sauce with veal stock and serve in a lovely dish alongside juicy beef or pork steaks. Don't forget the buttermilk biscuits for sopping up the extra sauce.

Chive Beurre Blanc

Looking for a sauce that won't overpower the naturally delicious flavors of your dish? Mild chives and smooth butter are your answer.

PREP TIME: 15 MINUTES

1/2 cup dry white wine

Pinch of sugar

1/4 teaspoon salt

1 cup cold unsalted butter, cubed

1 tablespoon chopped fresh chives

In a saucepan over high heat, bring the wine to a boil. Decrease the heat to medium and let simmer until reduced by half.

Season with sugar and salt. Decrease the heat to low and begin whisking in the cold butter cubes a little bit at a time, making sure that each addition is well incorporated before adding the next. The sauce should thicken to the consistency of a thick vinai-grette. Gently mix in the chives and serve immediately.

Variation: For an interesting variation in texture as well as flavor, mix 2 teaspoons salmon caviar into this sauce just before serving.

Serving Suggestions

This sauce is very good with delicate-flavored fish; strong-flavored fish will overpower its subtle flavor. It is particularly good with salmon, prepared any way you like.

I like to serve this sauce drizzled around slices of salmon pâté, garnished with salmon or beluga caviar.

Clarified Butter

French cuisine makes extensive use of clarified butter, as opposed to regular butter or oils. Basically, the clarification process separates the three components of which butter is composed: water, milk solids, and the clear, golden liquid that is the clarified butter. Its primary advantage in cooking is that it can be heated to much higher temperatures than regular butter or oils without burning, smoking, or browning, which means you can fry any and all of your foods to golden perfection every time—absolutely worry-free. The disadvantage, however, is that most of the deep, rich, wonderful flavor and aroma of butter is contained in the milk solids, which are usually discarded once separated from the clarified butter. You can cut that unfortunate loss by reserving the separated solids and using them in pastries and other dishes to enhance them with particularly concentrated, rich buttery flavor.

PREP TIME: 20 TO 30 MINUTES

2 cups unsalted butter

In a heavy saucepan over low heat, slowly melt the butter, occasionally skimming off the foam that rises to the surface. When you've skimmed off all the foam, you'll see a layer of white milky liquids and solids at the bottom of the pan through the clear, golden liquid on the surface. At this point, remove the pan from the heat and let cool for several minutes at room temperature.

Once slightly cool, separate the clarified butter from the milk solids by simply pouring off the golden liquid into a jar. The milk solids will remain at the bottom of the pan. (Spoon them up and save them, too.)

In an airtight jar, the butter will keep 3 to 4 days at room temperature. If you refrigerate it, it will turn hard as a rock, but you can keep it this way for much, much longer. Just let it soften at room temperature before using or, if frying in it, simply spoon out a chunk and toss it in the hot pan to melt. The milk solids are more perishable and will last only 1 to 2 days in an airtight jar in the refrigerator.

Variation: Instead of cooling and separating out the clarified butter as soon as you see the milk solids, continue heating the butter over low heat until the solid layer at the bottom of the saucepan turns golden. Remove from heat and immediately pour off the liquid at the top into a jar. The golden dairy solids will remain in the saucepan, and the clarified butter will reveal to you butter's best-kept secret: its essence of lovely, roasted nut flavor.

Serving Suggestions

Use clarified butter to fry chicken, hash browns, french fries, hamburgers, seafood, breaded vegetables, doughnuts, and more.

Making gumbo? Thicken it with a classic roux made with clarified butter. Make a little extra roux to use in your French dishes, as well as to thicken sauces, soups, and stews. The best hollandaise sauces are made with clarified butter; it requires the same amount as regular butter, but it helps keep the sauce together longer.

Before baking filet mignon, sear it in clarified butter until brown, then transfer it to the oven and cook until done.

The leftover milk solids taste great melted over very low heat and drizzled over pancakes, waffles, crêpes, and desserts.

For a delicious snack, preheat the oven to 475°F. Melt the leftover milk solids slowly over low heat

and brush onto readymade puff pastry dough. Cut the dough into strips, and sprinkle with coarse salt, caraway seeds, fennel seeds, sesame seeds, and coarsely ground chili powder. Bake for 5 to 7 minutes, until golden brown.

For extra buttery shortbread pastry or butter cookies, add 1 tablespoon milk solids (in addition to the amount of regular butter called for) to enough dough for 12 to 24 cookies. Or, knead 2 tablespoons milk solids into your muffin mix or enough readymade yeast dough for 12 to 24 rolls, and bake according to the package's directions.

Ethiopian Spiced Clarified Butter

Usually, butter is clarified for general cooking purposes, and so no flavors or spices are added. In this recipe, however, the butter is simultaneously clarified and strongly flavored with an Ethiopian spice combination.

PREP TIME: 60 MINUTES

1 cup unsalted butter

1 onion, chopped

3 tablespoons minced garlic

$1/4$ cup peeled and minced fresh ginger

2 teaspoons ground turmeric

$1/2$ teaspoon ground cinnamon

$1/4$ teaspoon ground nutmeg

$1/8$ teaspoon ground cloves

$1/8$ teaspoon ground cardamom

In a large saucepan over low heat, combine all ingredients and bring to a simmer. Let simmer for 40 minutes, skimming off any foam that rises to the surface with a slotted spoon. Remove from heat and let cool for 10 minutes in the pan.

Strain the sauce through a very fine-mesh sieve or a piece of cheesecloth. Discard whatever remains in the sieve. Pour the strained butter into an airtight jar and store in the refrigerator.

Serving Suggestions

An excellent butter for cooking: just replace any oil or fat called for in a recipe with the spiced butter for an aromatic and flavorful result. Begin any stir-fry by sautéing the vegetables in this butter or start off soups and stews by browning the meats in it.

Try drizzling the hot butter on soups and warm salads. Top those same soups and salads with exotically spiced croutons: simply drizzle the butter over 2 cups fresh bread cubes and bake in an oven preheated to 350°F for 5 to 7 minutes, until golden.

Lemon-Mustard Butter Sauce

Citrus and seed, tang and spice—whatever you love this combination in already, you can enhance even more with this butter sauce. Butter adds smooth, fresh dairy to the sharp flavors of this favorite American combo.

PREP TIME: 10 TO 15 MINUTES

1/4 cup stock

1/4 cup dry white wine

1 teaspoon freshly squeezed lemon juice

Grated zest of 1/2 lemon

2 teaspoons prepared mustard

Generous pinch of salt

Pinch of sugar

5 1/2 tablespoons cold unsalted butter, cubed

1 tablespoon chopped fresh parsley (optional)

In a saucepan over high heat, bring the stock and wine to a boil and let cook until reduced by two-thirds. Add the lemon juice and zest, mustard, salt, and sugar and whisk well. Decrease the heat to low and begin whisking in the butter, one cube at a time, making sure that each addition is well incorporated before adding the next. The sauce should thicken considerably. Whisk in the parsley, if using, just before serving. Serve immediately.

Serving Suggestions

A divine accompaniment to steaks, ribs, veal scallops, fish fillets, and chicken breasts.

If you are preparing your meat or fish in a skillet, it's a good idea to prepare the sauce in the same skillet in order to get all the rich flavors into the sauce. Simply discard all the fat after cooking your meat or fish and start making your sauce without washing the skillet.

Maple-Pecan Butter Sauce

I used to use a strictly sweet variation of this recipe quite a lot when baking cakes and cookies, until I created this version for roasting. The plain sweet one was pretty good, but every time I roast with this sauce my guests won't leave until I give them the recipe. The magic of it is its unusually thick, heavy texture, which makes it practically the all-purpose sauce: refrigerated it can be used as a spread, at room temperature it makes a great syrup, and slightly heated it can be drizzled or brushed onto a variety of dishes. If you want to try the sweet butter in your baked goods as well, just leave out the soy sauce. The unique blend of flavors in this version tastes best in sweet and savory dishes.

PREP TIME: 30 MINUTES

1 cup unsalted butter, softened

1/2 cup pecans

1/4 cup pure maple syrup

2 tablespoons soy sauce

In a frying pan over medium heat, melt 1 tablespoon of the butter. Add the pecans and sauté, stirring occasionally, for about 5 minutes, or until golden.

Add the maple syrup and cook for 4 minutes. Add the soy sauce and cook for 4 minutes more. Remove from heat and let cool in the pan for about 15 minutes, or until the mixture reaches room temperature.

Using a rubber spatula, scrape the pecans and syrup into a food processor fitted with a metal blade. Add the remaining butter and process in short bursts, just until well combined. Do not let the butter become a smooth paste.

Serve immediately or refrigerate for up to 1 week. (Best used within 4 days.)

Serving Suggestions

Serve dolloped onto your hot pancakes in the morning. Let the butter melt slightly and add more syrup if desired.

Brush slightly melted butter onto ready-made puff pastry, cut into narrow strips, and bake into fabulous sweet and savory pecan treats.

Brush a thick layer of room-temperature sauce onto spareribs, leg of lamb, or chicken wings, then barbecue or broil until cooked through.

Mustard-Horseradish Butter Sauce

Mustard and horseradish are actually from the same family of plants, hence their similarly distinctive, sharp, fresh tastes. Combined, they make a divine fish sauce, but this butter sauce can also be served with meat or poultry.

PREP TIME: 15 MINUTES

$1/2$ **cup dry white wine**

$1/2$ **cup stock**

1 bay leaf, crushed

1 shallot, chopped

4 whole peppercorns

2 sprigs parsley

1 level tablespoon good-quality prepared mustard

1 level tablespoon freshly grated horseradish

$1/2$ **cup cold unsalted butter, diced**

In a saucepan, bring the wine, stock, bay leaf, shallot, peppercorns, parsley, mustard, and horseradish to a boil. Simmer rapidly over high heat until the mixture reduces by two-thirds.

Strain through a fine-mesh sieve; discard the solids that remain in the sieve and pour the strained liquid back into the saucepan.

Over low heat, begin whisking the butter into the mixture in small amounts, making sure each addition is well incorporated before adding the next.

Taste and adjust the seasoning. The mixture will begin to separate with overheating (or even if just left to stand for a few minutes), so once you have the seasoning just right, pour the sauce over the dish for which it was intended and serve immediately.

Serving Suggestions

Pour over whole poached or steamed fish. Or try frying fish fillets on the skin side only until the meat is cooked through and the skin very crisp, then serve with this sauce and some pasta or rice on the side.

Pour over any type of grilled, baked, or broiled meat or poultry. Full-flavored, rich meats, such as roast beef and smoked ham, are especially delicious drenched in this sauce.

Port Wine Butter Sauce

Sauces made with port have a very subtle sweetness that naturally enhances full, meaty flavors. Use such a sauce to upgrade just about any meat meal, or to make a truly festive dinner for guests. Though port sauces are generally best with meats, they also make great accompaniments to lobster and scallops, as these both have quite meaty flavor and texture.

PREP TIME: 20 TO 30 MINUTES

1/2 **cup port**

1/2 **cup stock**

4 whole peppercorns

2 shallots, chopped

2 sprigs parsley

Generous pinch of salt

1/2 **cup cold unsalted butter, cubed**

In a saucepan over high heat, bring the port, stock, peppercorns, shallots, parsley, and salt to a boil and let boil until reduced by two-thirds.

Remove from heat and strain through a fine-mesh sieve. Discard what remains in the sieve and return the strained liquid to the saucepan.

Over very low heat, begin whisking in the butter cubes a little bit at a time, making sure each addition is well incorporated before adding the next.

Taste and adjust the seasoning. The sauce will begin to separate if overheated (or even if only left to stand for a few minutes), so as soon as you have the seasoning just right, pour the sauce over your dish and serve.

Serving Suggestions

This is the classic sauce for veal scaloppine. Or slice pork loin very thin, dredge in flour, and fry in a buttered skillet for just 1 minute on each side. Serve with this fine sauce poured over top or in a dish on the side.

Pour over thin slices of braised turkey or pork. Be sure to serve with thick slices of bread for soaking up every last drop of sauce.

Soy Sauce, Honey, and Cilantro Butter Sauce

This sauce is one of my favorites because the mild sweetness of the honey moderates the sharpness of the chili powder, but competes with the saltiness of the broth. It's also an excellent sauce for dieters because it's very strong in flavor, so you only need a small amount on any dish. If you don't generally like this sort of sweet and savory combination, this sauce will change your mind.

PREP TIME: 10 TO 15 MINUTES

³/₄ cup cold unsalted butter, diced

1 large clove garlic, crushed

¹/₄ teaspoon chili powder

1 cup stock

3 tablespoons honey

1 tablespoon soy sauce

1 tablespoon chopped fresh cilantro

Freshly milled black pepper

In a saucepan over medium heat, melt 1 tablespoon of the butter. Add the garlic and sauté for 1 minute, or until golden. Add the chili powder and sauté for 1 more minute.

Pour in the stock and honey and bring to a boil over high heat, then decrease the heat to medium and simmer until reduced by half.

Add the soy sauce, cilantro, and black pepper and simmer for 1 more minute.

Decrease the heat to low and begin whisking in the remaining butter a little bit at a time, making sure that each addition is well incorporated before adding the next. When all the butter has been mixed in, taste and adjust the seasoning. Serve immediately.

Serving Suggestions

This gorgeous sauce is truly versatile and matches almost any dish. Try it on all your roasted or grilled beef, venison, pork, and poultry.

You can use fish stock in this recipe and pour the resulting sauce over all types of fish and seafood, both before and after cooking.

Tangy Mediterranean Butter Sauce

This sauce screams southern Europe as its many Mediterranean flavors explode in your mouth. Each ingredient is important to the overall harmony of flavors. Herbes de Provence is a dried mixture of the herbs most popular in southern France. You can find this blend in tiny little jars or clay crocks at the supermarket or in specialty food stores.

PREP TIME: 15 MINUTES

1 scallion, white and green parts, thinly sliced

3 shallots, chopped

1 tablespoon olive oil

1/2 cup stock

1 teaspoon balsamic vinegar

1 tablespoon drained and finely sliced oil-packed sun-dried tomatoes

1 tablespoon finely chopped black olives

1 tablespoon finely chopped fresh flat-leaf parsley

1/2 teaspoon herbes de Provence

1 clove garlic, crushed

Generous pinch of salt

Freshly milled black pepper

1/2 cup cold unsalted butter, cubed

In a saucepan over medium heat, sauté the scallion and shallots in the oil for 3 to 4 minutes, until translucent.

Add the stock, increase the heat to high, and boil rapidly for about 5 minutes, or until the liquid is reduced by half.

Decrease the heat to low and add the vinegar, sun-dried tomatoes, olives, parsley, herbes de Provence, garlic, salt, and pepper.

Whisk in the butter cubes one at a time, making sure each addition is well incorporated before adding the next. The sauce should thicken considerably and emit a mouth-watering aroma. Serve immediately.

Serving Suggestions

Try this sauce poured over a medium-done steak with a side of mashed potatoes for a simple yet not-quite-ordinary dinner.

Pour generously over cooked lobster or sautéed scampi and remember to serve plenty of fresh bread for dipping.

Tarragon-Honey Butter Sauce

This sauce was a favorite in one of the restaurants I used to manage. It belonged to a dish of turkey scaloppine, which we tried to replace now and then to keep the menu new and interesting. It was so popular that guests demanded it back every time, and eventually we just gave up. Now I give it to you and of course recommend that you try it poured onto turkey scaloppine.

PREP TIME: 5 TO 10 MINUTES

3/4 cup cold unsalted butter, diced

1 clove garlic, crushed

3 tablespoons honey

1 cup stock

1/4 teaspoon salt

1 tablespoon chopped fresh tarragon

Freshly milled black pepper

In a saucepan over medium heat, melt 1 tablespoon of the butter. Add the garlic and sauté 1 minute, until pale golden. Add the honey and let simmer for 2 to 3 minutes, just until it begins to darken a little in color.

Pour in the stock and salt and bring to a boil over high heat. Let simmer rapidly until reduced by half.

Decrease the heat to low and begin whisking in the remaining butter a little bit at a time, making sure that each addition is well incorporated before adding the next.

Add the tarragon and a generous pinch of black pepper. Taste and adjust the seasoning. Serve immediately.

Serving Suggestions

To make turkey scaloppine, slice turkey very, very thinly, dredge it in flour, and fry in a buttered pan over medium heat for about 2 minutes on each side, until golden. Pour on the sauce and serve.

In truth, you can slice just about any meat very thinly and dip it in this sauce or pour it over the slices themselves. The result is mouth-watering, and people never seem to get tired of it. Try it on sautéed, grilled, and barbecued meats and on poached, boiled, fried, and steamed fish and seafood.

White Wine Butter Sauce

This recipe is a must in every gourmet's kitchen. Be sure to select very good-quality wine for excellent results. The color of the butter—from deep yellow to pale white—will determine the color of your sauce.

PREP TIME: 15 MINUTES

1 cup good-quality dry white wine

$1/4$ cup chopped shallots

1 teaspoon whole peppercorns

1 bay leaf (optional)

$1/4$ cup cold unsalted butter, cubed

$1/4$ teaspoon salt

Pinch of sugar

2 tablespoons heavy cream (optional)

In a saucepan over high heat, bring the wine, shallots, peppercorns, and bay leaf to a boil. Let simmer until reduced by two-thirds.

Strain the liquid through a fine-mesh sieve. Return the strained liquid to the saucepan; discard the solids that remain in the sieve.

Over low heat, begin whisking in the butter, one cube at a time, making sure that each addition is well incorporated before adding the next. The sauce should become quite thick.

Add the salt and sugar. If using cream, whisk it in at this stage.

Variations: If you are intending to serve the sauce on fish or chicken, add $1/2$ cup fish or chicken stock with the wine to enrich the seafood or poultry flavor of the entire dish.

Stir in 1 tablespoon chives just before serving to give the sauce a little kick.

To keep the sauce interesting, add a little distinctive character to it every time by mixing in parsley, fennel, garlic, cilantro, or other fresh herbs and spices just before serving.

Serving Suggestions

No veal scaloppine is complete without a white wine sauce. This one adds buttery richness to veal's natural tenderness as well.

It is excellent on braised or poached fish, white meat cuts such as pork or milk-fed veal chops, chicken, and stuffed turkey breast.